T0306592

Assessing the Needs of Soldiers and Their Families at the Garrison Level

Carra S. Sims, Thomas E. Trail, Emily K. Chen, Erika Meza, Parisa Roshan, Beth E. Lachman

Prepared for the United States Army

For more information on this publication, visit www.rand.org/t/RR2148

Library of Congress Cataloging-in-Publication Data is available for this publication.
ISBN: 978-0-8330-9912-9

Support RAND
Make a tax-deductible charitable contribution at
www.rand.org/giving/contribute

www.rand.org

Preface

This report documents research and analysis conducted as part of a project entitled *Assessing the Needs of Soldiers at the Garrison Level*, sponsored by the Assistant Chief of Staff for Installation Management, Installation Management Command. The purpose of this project was to analyze existing survey data at the garrison level and gathering additional qualitative data from focus groups in order to gain a fuller understanding of the effect of garrison-level variations on quality-of-life support services for soldiers and their families.

The Project Unique Identification Code (PUIC) for the project that produced this document is RAN167279.

This research was conducted within RAND Arroyo Center's Personnel, Training and Health Program. RAND Arroyo Center, part of the RAND Corporation, is a federally funded research and development center (FFRDC) sponsored by the United States Army.

RAND operates under a "Federal-Wide Assurance" (FWA00003425) and complies with the *Code of Federal Regulations for the Protection of Human Subjects Under United States Law* (45 CFR 46), also known as "the Common Rule," as well as with the implementation guidance set forth in DoD Instruction 3216.02. As applicable, this compliance includes reviews and approvals by RAND's Institutional Review Board (the Human Subjects Protection Committee) and by the U.S. Army. The views of sources utilized in this study are solely their own and do not represent the official policy or position of DoD or the U.S. government.

Contents

Figures

Tables

Summary

Background

The U.S. Army makes many demands of its members and, inevitably, their families. A constant cycle of overseas deployments, coupled with the frequent moves that are inherent in military life, places a lot of strain on soldiers and families. The Army has established a wide range of programs to help soldiers and their families cope with the many issues and problems of military life (e.g., deployment cycles). However, it has not always been clear whether these programs meet the most pressing needs of soldiers and their families and help them resolve their problems. To assess the match between Army programs and the needs of soldiers and their families, researchers from the RAND Arroyo Center designed a broad-ranging survey that considered the installation environment, the demographics of the population, the problems encountered, the types of help needed as a result of those problems, the resources soldiers draw on to deal with the problems, the barriers to using both military and civilian resources to meet needs, the effectiveness of the resources used, and, last, attitudes toward military service. That survey, administered to over 7,000 soldiers from September 2014 to January 2015, and the report that followed (Sims, Trail, et al., 2017) took an Army-wide view of how its members used the resources provided to them and whether there were gaps between the perceived needs of soldiers and their families for dealing with problems and the resources available to help with those problems.

Purpose and Approach

Many of the conditions that affect soldiers depend on the local context. Life at an Army post near a major metropolitan center such as Fort Meade, Maryland, differs from one located in a sparsely populated rural area such as Fort Huachuca, Arizona, especially for issues such as housing options. Thus, it is likely that issues confronting soldiers and their families also differ, certainly in degree and possibly in kind. While the Sims, Trail, et al. (2017) report helps the Army determine whether its resources are accomplishing their intended purpose, a more local-level analysis is necessary to determine whether the overall perspective masks local patterns of disparate problems, needs, or resource use.

This report presents this type of analysis: it digs more deeply into what resources soldiers and family members use and provides additional insight into questions raised by the survey. The goal was to understand how soldiers' and families' perceived problems and strategies to cope with them might vary across installations.

This study took a mixed-methods approach to examine soldier and family problems, needs, and resource use at the garrison level. One component of the research used existing survey data from soldiers. The second component used site visits to selected installations as the data source. This mixed-methods approach offers the benefits of more generalizable analysis (i.e., quantitative survey analysis) married with analysis more suited to uncovering processes and local variance (i.e., focus groups and interviews). We were also able to gather the perspectives of spouses and service providers on the challenges faced by soldiers and families, and how they deal with them.

We analyzed survey data from the following 13 garrisons[1] to identify the problems soldiers and their family members encountered, the needs those problems generated, and the resources used to deal with the problems:

- Fort Bragg
- Fort Campbell
- Fort Eustis
- Fort Gordon
- Fort Hood
- Fort Huachuca
- Fort Jackson
- Fort Knox
- Fort Leavenworth
- Fort Meade
- Fort Polk
- Fort Rucker
- Fort Sill.

For survey analyses, we compared the selected garrisons to the *overall average* of all garrisons in the larger sample of 40 installations within the continental United States (CONUS), including those with too few unweighted respondents to be selected for more in-depth study. In addition to our analysis of previously collected survey data, we gathered additional in-depth information through focus groups with soldiers, Army spouses, and service providers at four installations. All told, over 4,500 people from the selected garrisons participated in our survey, interviews, and focus groups.

How to Use This Report

In our findings, areas where there are similarities across garrisons suggest problems, needs, and resource use patterns that require an Army-wide approach to address. Areas

[1] We selected the garrisons that had at least 200 unweighted survey responses for further analysis. A respondent size of 200 was estimated to be the minimum number to provide for a variety of garrisons for analysis while maintaining enough respondents to allow for statistical analysis.

where there are differences across garrisons suggest that the local context plays a role in the challenges soldiers and their families face. Differences among garrisons might suggest that a local solution is needed or that the local context, including initiatives by leaders, may help soldiers and their families successfully address the challenges they face. The comprehensive and systematic approach taken by the survey enables leaders to make decisions about garrison needs and priorities based on empirical data describing the Army population. This study provides unique information that enables service providers and garrison leadership to understand where they are doing well in relation to other surveyed garrisons, where their communities still report experiencing challenges in addressing their most pressing problems effectively, and where additional effort might be warranted.

The Survey

The survey sample consisted of active component enlisted soldiers and officers stationed at CONUS installations. Survey respondents received a list of 83 individual issues, which were grouped into nine problem domains that they could indicate they had experienced in the past year. The problem domains (with examples of specific issues) are as follows:

- **Military Practices and Culture** (e.g., problems adjusting to military language, organization, culture; lack of guidance or sponsorship)
- **Work/Life Balance** (e.g., finding time for sleep, a healthy diet, and physical exercise; finding time for education; nearby and affordable options for stress relief and family time)
- **Household Management** (e.g., finding suitable housing, time management)
- **Financial or Legal Problems** (e.g., trouble paying debt or bills, child custody/family legal problems)
- **Health Care System** (e.g., getting access to military health care, understanding military health benefits)
- **Relationship Problems** (e.g., problems communicating/expressing feelings, trouble starting a relationship)
- **Child Well-Being** (e.g., childcare problems, child emotional/behavior problems)
- **Soldier's Own Well-Being** (e.g., feeling stressed, overwhelmed, or tired; dealing with mood changes, including anxiety and depression)
- **Spouse's Well-Being** (e.g., feeling stressed, overwhelmed, or tired; dealing with mood changes, including anxiety and depression)
- **Other Problems** (write in responses).

After indicating which problems they had encountered in the last year, respondents were prompted to choose two problems that were the most important or troubling, the "top-two" problems.

Next, each survey respondent was asked to indicate what types of help, if any, he or she needed to deal with the top two specific problems in that domain. The list of types of help was the same for all problem domains and included needs such as "general information," "an advocate: someone to try to get help for you," and "professional counseling." If respondents listed more than two types of help needed for any problem, they were asked to choose the top two types of needs for the problem. The goal of this approach was to generate a sense of whether the types of help typically offered reflected the types of help typically desired, independent of specific resources for assistance.

Then, for each respondent's need, we asked him or her to indicate which resources, if any, he or she had used or tried to use to address the need. The list of resources was the same for all problem domains and needs, and included both Army (e.g., Army Community Service [ACS] or chain of command) and nonmilitary (e.g., private off-post childcare or personal networks of friends and family) resources. For each resource a participant indicated that he or she contacted, he or she was asked to rate "how well each of these contacts you made helped to meet your needs" for each of the top-two problems.

What We Found from the Survey Data

Generally, the top three problems identified in the garrison analysis mirrored those of the Army-wide survey: Military Practices and Culture, Work-Life Balance, and the Soldier's Well-Being. Although the problem domains most frequently chosen were largely the same across garrisons, there was significant variance in the selection of some specific problem domains. For example, compared to the average, Health Care System Problems was more frequently chosen as a top problem by respondents at Fort Meade, and it was ranked as one of the top three problems chosen by Fort Meade respondents. Similarly, Work-Life Balance ranked as a top concern for almost all garrisons, but it was chosen more frequently at Fort Hood, compared with the average. Thus, although our findings illustrated that certain problems are typical, regardless of location, some significant variation in the prevalence of these problems occurred across garrisons.

Also, more variance appeared in the types of help needed to solve problems. Advice, activities, and general information were still seen as highly prioritized sources of help, but the additional need for interpersonal help in the form of counseling, emotional support, and an advocate were cited at some posts. The top problem-need pairings at installations had many similarities with the Army-wide data.

In terms of how effective resources were in solving problems, military resources were widely used to help. However, garrisons varied on which resources were used most frequently. Furthermore, with the exception of Fort Leavenworth, where soldiers used fewer Army resources than average, the number of Army and nonmilitary resources did not differ by garrison. When resources were used to address problems, fewer than 20 percent of respondents at any garrison reported that their needs were unmet (that is, that the resources that they reached out for met their needs in a manner rated less than "all right"), and, compared to the average, soldiers at Fort Polk were less likely to report unmet needs.

Focus Groups and Interviews

We chose garrisons for site visits based on the pattern of survey results by respondents at each garrison across a set of important outcomes: the number and type of problems, the needs reported, the types of resources used, and the percentage of soldiers at the garrison who had unmet needs (that is, all resources used in attempting to address a given problem and need were rated as meeting the need less than "well"). Based on those criteria, we visited four installations: Fort Gordon, Georgia; Fort Hood, Texas; Fort Huachuca, Arizona; and Fort Meade, Maryland. We conducted 12 interviews and 40 focus groups across the installations. None of these installations could be said to be reflective of the average Army garrison, if there is such a thing; all were unique in some way. For example, the missions and duties of soldiers stationed at Forts Gordon, Huachuca, and Meade make gaining and retaining appropriate security clearances of paramount importance for soldiers; Fort Hood is the largest active-duty armored post in the United States. Garrisons were chosen based on their survey profile rather than other characteristics.

In focus groups, we provided participants with a list of the problem categories (with examples) that were used in the survey and asked them what were the most common or most pressing problems soldiers and their families were facing. The top problems cited were the following:

- Soldier Well-Being
- Military Practices and Culture
- Work-Life Balance
- Health Care System
- Childcare.

Thus, focus groups identified a somewhat different emphasis, or prioritization, of problems from that identified in the survey. These differences included a greater emphasis on childcare and housing; issues with soldier well-being, including work-related stress (a result of short staff); feelings of isolation and disconnectedness or lack of unit cohesion; working on operational missions while in garrison; and unhealthy diets. From the soldier perspective, the main issue with military practices and culture was a lack of proper guidance or sponsorship. From the leaders' perspective, the main issues with military practices and culture were that soldiers had poor communication with their supervisors and that the many responsibilities piled on leaders took time away from mentoring opportunities.

Focus groups also revealed the interconnected nature of problems. Problems with work-life balance such as the "24-hour Army" and a need to do more with less spilled over into Soldier Well-Being, because a lack of time made it difficult to manage a home life and make as much progress as desired with regard to professional life. Military Practices and Culture challenges exacerbated these issues: as more requirements were piled on, they were seen as contributing to a lack of time to develop relationships with soldiers and foster the ability to provide advice.

Several key themes emerged about health care systems. Lack of direct or convenient access to providers was cited frequently, and causes included a burdensome and invasive triage process and extensive travel time. Long wait times for appointments (often over a month) were also cited and attributed to inadequate system capacity. Concerns were also voiced about malingerers who were avoiding duty by gaming the health care system (and also absorbing capacity) and, on the flip side, were suspected of faking injury or illness. Unsurprisingly, some complaints were installation specific. For example, at Fort Meade, the travel time to medical facilities, which were often not on post, was perceived to be inordinately long. At Fort Huachuca, the lack of on-post facilities and the burden of getting into off-post facilities were cited.

Nearly all of the problems cited with childcare focused on day care. The long wait times for access to Child Development Centers were cited, and having to wait to access childcare was particularly frustrating for dual-military couples and single parents. Operating hours were an additional topic, with soldiers noting that they did not always mesh well with the military work schedules, either closing too early or opening too late.

The focus group findings indicate a culture of self-sufficiency, and accessibility of resources in terms of hours, location, and approachability was noted as both a facilitator and a barrier. ACS and chaplains were the most consistently cited sources for successfully meeting needs, and ACS and noncommissioned officers (NCOs) were recognized as the primary options for seeking help.

What We Recommend

In considering how best to manage challenges faced by soldiers and families while maintaining readiness, the Army should strike a balance between solving problems and supporting resilience. Complex, interrelated problems can demand an array of resources. The Army should support resources that can provide general support for a range of common problems and that can link soldiers with specialized resources when needed. Soldiers at all levels often reported that they wanted to be able—or should be able—to solve their problems themselves without needing to bring leadership into the equation. That sentiment was balanced by the responses of NCOs who expressed a sense of responsibility for their soldiers, along with an awareness that soldiers might wish to maintain their privacy. Respondents pointed out that the downside of this tension can be that, by the time individuals realize they are in over their heads and need assistance, their challenges have evolved into a much knottier problem to untangle.

To manage these ongoing challenges, the Army may consider several options:

- Early in their career, expose NCOs and other leaders to information they need to help soldiers navigate the system more consistently.
- Give priority for time for NCOs to develop relationships with their soldiers. These priorities should be set at the Army-wide level rather than leaving it up to individual leaders to set their own priorities among their many tasks.
- Increase interpersonal help such as counseling and advocacy services at specific installations.
- Explore community partnerships that help meet soldier and family needs, following partnership best practices discussed in this report.
- If the budgets for resources that serve as gateways or connectors to other resources must be trimmed or cut completely, stipulate that alternative gateways to resources must be established as a substitute. Strengthening and broadening ACS's "no wrong door" policy might prove advantageous to facilitating navigation through the resource environment as well.

Finally and more specifically, our survey findings suggest a greater need for an advocate at Meade. More generally, information and advice were widely prioritized across installations, which suggests the importance of continuing to provide easily accessible information online, for example (as this was reported as one of the primary sources used to find information on what is available), and continuing to staff services that provide information and advice to soldiers.

Acknowledgments

We thank our sponsor, Ms. Diane M. Randon, deputy assistant chief of staff for installation management, for comments and guidance on this research. We would also like to thank our action officer, Dr. Richard Fafara. We also are grateful to Joseph Trebing and Kelly (Dorie) Hickson of Soldier and Family Readiness (DAIM-ISS), Office of the Assistant Chief of Staff for Installation Management, Installation Services, who provided invaluable help with fielding the survey emails, coordinating with other stakeholders, and connecting us with appropriate points of contact for qualitative data collection, as well as providing thoughtful feedback.

Many individuals contributed to adapting and improving the suitability of survey instruments for use in the Army, through thoughtful feedback and formal pretesting. In addition to the support of our action officers, we benefited from the involvement of Tracey Anbiya (Assistant Secretary of the Army for Installations, Energy & Environment), Jeffrey Hartless (Installation Management Command), and soldiers at Fort Meade, as well as Kayla Williams, Philip Padilla, and Lily Geyer, RAND Arroyo Center Fellows, and Pardee RAND Graduate School students. David Stebbins helped manage the constant edits to the offline version of the survey. Terry West programmed the survey.

We want to thank our contacts at Installation Management Command and at the individual installations we visited who made our data collection a success. These include (but are not limited to) Ms. Mary Staab (director of the Directorate of Plans, Training, Mobilization and Security [DPTMS]) at Fort Meade, Mr. Dale Cowan (program management analyst with the Plans, Analysis and Integration Office) at Fort Hood, Mr. Bradley Branderhorst (operations officer in DPTMS) at Fort Huachuca, and Ms. Jane Barnard (director of the Soldier and Family Assistance Center) at Fort Gordon. We also have to thank the soldiers, family members, and Family Readiness Group members who patiently answered our questions. Many service providers also patiently answered our questions and in some cases took time out of their busy days to show us their facilities and explain their perspective on how they support soldiers and what challenges soldiers and families face.

Jeff Hiday and James Gazis provided assistance with the RAND portion of the outreach to potential participants. Bernie Rostker and Laura Miller gave us feedback on conceptual issues and general project mentorship. Beth Lachman also provided thoughtful feedback throughout the study, as well as supporting our qualitative data collection efforts with a particular focus on partnerships. Bonnie Ghosh-Dastidar and Robin Beckman provided statistical advice and expert consultation.

At RAND, we also thank Michael Hansen, the director of the Personnel, Training, and Health Program, for his guidance and advice, as well as Shanthi Nataraj, associate director of the Personnel, Training, and Health Program; Jerry Sollinger for his editorial help; and Martha Friese, Kat Mariska, and Lemenuel Dungey for administrative assistance. Last but certainly not least, we would like to thank our reviewers, Sarah Meadows and Mady Segal, for their thoughtful suggestions on how to improve this report.

Abbreviations

ACS	Army Community Service
AER	Army Emergency Relief
CDC	Child Development Center
CONUS	continental United States
FAP	Family Advocacy Program
FRG	Family Readiness Group
MWR	Morale, Welfare, and Recreation
NCO	noncommissioned officer
OSD	Office of the Secretary of Defense
PT	physical training

CHAPTER ONE

Introduction

Background and Purpose

U.S. military personnel and their families face a variety of stresses related to features of military life, such as frequent moves and deployments. These deployments include combat deployments around the world, which separate military members from their families and place additional stress on family members at risk. Ideally, service members are able to stay focused on the mission, but, as with all jobs, at times life gets in the way. Given the military necessity for deployable military members, these outside problems can have untoward influence on an individual's ability to deploy, and that may have a ripple effect within units, as unit resources—for example, the time and attention of noncommissioned and commissioned leaders—may be required to resolve problems. More prosaically, challenges within the personal realm may influence general well-being and morale and retention intentions.

The Army provides an array of quality-of-life support services for soldiers and their families and has long been interested in their well-being and quality of life (for reviews of research in this domain over time, see Segal and Harris, 1993; McClure, 1999; and Booth, Segal, and Bell, 2007); these issues are also subjects of interest at the level of the Department of Defense (see, for example, the 2004 and 2009 quadrennial quality of life reviews, Office of the Secretary of Defense [OSD], 2004; and OSD, 2009). Aside from such broad overviews and reviews of research, other work has delved more deeply into specific areas of concern such as child well-being (see, for example, Bello-Utu and DeSocio, 2015) or the quality of the health care soldiers and families receive (e.g., Jennings et al., 2005; Military Health System, 2014; Wong and Gerras, 2015). Still more specific well-being issues include sleep quality (Troxel et al., 2015) and the health of Army spouses experiencing the deployment of their partners (Mansfield et al., 2010).[1] Despite this wealth of research and inquiry, the Army until recently has lacked a holistic assessment of problems soldiers and families face and what types of

---

[1] For a more detailed review of the available literature on Army programs, and the problems and needs of soldiers and families, see Sims, Trail, et al., 2017.

assistance they perceive as needed to resolve those problems (Sims, Wong, et al., 2013; Sims, Trail, et al., 2017).

Information on these issues was collected by means of an Army-wide survey of 7,000 soldiers at 40 garrisons and was recently reported on at the aggregate Army level (Sims, Trail, et al., 2017). However, as acknowledged in that report, the types of resources available to soldiers and families to solve problems, especially resources in the civilian sector, are intrinsically local. To the extent that local influences can fuel some types of problems (e.g., the availability of childcare), and the large majority of Army resources are delivered locally, problems and their solutions occur at the garrison rather than "big Army" level. Engaging soldiers and their families at the local level provides a unique understanding of local variance in problems, needs, and resource use. Hence, while the initial high-level report helps the Army determine whether the Army resources in place and consistently offered are doing the job they are intended for (Sims, Trail, et al., 2017), a more garrison-level analysis is necessary to determine whether the overall perspective masks local patterns. This report presents that analysis. It delves more deeply into what resources soldiers and family members use and how they access them, and it provides additional insight into questions raised by the survey. The goal was to understand how problems and strategies to cope with them might vary across installations.

Analytical Approach

This study used a mixed-methods approach to examine soldier and family problems, needs, and resource use at the garrison level. One component of the research used existing survey data from soldiers only. The second component of the research relied on site visits to selected installations as the source of data about soldier and family problems and resource use. This qualitative component included focus groups with soldiers, as well as focus groups with Army spouses and focus groups and interviews with service providers.

This mixed-methods approach offers the benefits of more generalizable analysis (i.e., quantitative survey analysis), married with analysis more suited to uncovering processes and local variance (i.e., focus groups and interviews).

Our initial analysis of the survey results raised a number of questions that the current methods aim to address. These included questions surrounding the relatively high numbers of contacts sought when engaging with the resources available. Did these multiple contacts reflect an unsatisfactory trial-and-error process of help seeking, or were they the result of particularly complex problems? In addition, the focus group methodology provided an opportunity to engage with Army spouses directly to explore their problems and use of resources, particularly the use of Family Readiness Groups (FRGs). A final benefit of the qualitative component of this research was that engaging with local-level resource providers offered an opportunity to identify location-specific best practices.

How to Use This Report

Areas where there are differences across garrisons suggest that the local context plays a role in the challenges soldiers and their families face. Differences among garrisons might suggest that a local solution is needed or that the local context, including initiatives by leaders, may help soldiers and their families successfully address the challenges they face. The comprehensive and systematic approach taken by the survey enables leaders to make decisions about garrison needs and priorities based on empirical data describing the Army population. However, the survey information does not provide a fully contextualized explanation for garrison-related differences or suggest garrison-specific solutions, and, while our focus groups generated some explanations for challenges and some local best practices, they did not comprehensively explore all options. What this work does provide is information that enables service providers and garrison leadership to understand where they are doing well in relation to other surveyed garrisons. It also highlights where their communities still report experiencing challenges in addressing their most pressing problems effectively and where additional effort might be warranted.

How This Report Is Organized

This report has four chapters. Chapter Two describes our mixed-methods approach. It discusses the survey and the protocols for the site visit. It also discusses the caveats and limitations of our approach. Chapter Three presents the results of our analysis of the survey data gathered. It describes the number of issues we found by location and which were the most frequently cited problems. It also provides the results of our analysis of the focus groups, identifying the main problem domains and what was perceived as needed to deal with those problems. It also describes what resources were used and what the gateways were for those resources. The final chapter contains our recommendations. The Appendix contains our focus group protocol.

CHAPTER TWO

Mixed-Methods Approach

This chapter provides detail on the methodology for the soldier needs survey and the site visits that we used in our mixed-methods approach. We provide a brief description of our survey approach. Interested readers can find a more detailed presentation of the survey-related sampling, weighting, and analysis in Sims, Trail, et al. (2017). As the site visits and qualitative methodology are unique to this report, we cover them in more detail here.

Overview of Survey Methodology

Survey Instrument

This section offers an overview of the survey instrument; interested readers should refer to Sims, Trail, et al. (2017) for more information. Adapted from earlier work (Miller et al., 2011), the survey essentially parallels the coping process for dealing with problems: respondents are asked about problems they have faced, needs for help stemming from these problems, resources they have contacted for help, and the quality of their experience using resources. The diagram that follows illustrates this question flow:

Problems → Needs → Use of resources → Outcomes

Problems

Respondents received a list of nine problem domains, each with between 5 and 13 specific issues that they could indicate they had experienced in the past year. The problem domains (with examples of specific issues) appear here. The diversity of the problem areas presented in the survey is intended to reflect the wide range of challenges that arise for soldiers and their families.

- **Military Practices and Culture** (e.g., problems adjusting to military language, organization, culture; lack of guidance or sponsorship)
- **Work-Life Balance** (e.g., finding time for sleep, a healthy diet, and physical exercise; finding time for education; nearby and affordable options for stress relief and family time)

- **Household Management** (e.g., finding suitable housing, time management)
- **Financial or Legal Problems** (e.g., trouble paying debt or bills, child custody/family legal problems)
- **Health Care System** (e.g., getting access to military health care, understanding military health benefits)
- **Relationship Problems** (e.g., problems communicating/expressing feelings, trouble starting a relationship)
- **Child Well-Being** (e.g., childcare problems, child emotional/behavior problems)
- **Soldier's Own Well-Being** (e.g., feeling stressed, overwhelmed, or tired; dealing with mood changes, including anxiety and depression)
- **Spouse's Well-Being** (e.g., feeling stressed, overwhelmed, or tired; dealing with mood changes, including anxiety and depression)
- **Other Problems** (write in responses).

If respondents listed more than two issues overall, they were asked to choose the two "most significant problems" they faced in the past twelve months. All additional questions on the survey were asked about these "top two" problems. Note that the holistic approach taken in this study overall, with its broad range of problem domains, allows potential interrelatedness of problems to be more visible. Other surveys (in particular), which only ask about one or two of the problem domains, do not offer perspectives on the scope of potential interrelatedness.

Needs

For each respondent's top-two problems, he or she was asked to indicate what types of help, if any, were needed to deal with the specific problems in that domain. The list of types of help was the same for all problem domains and included the following options:

- General information: for example, about rules or policies, or about what is available and how to access it
- Specific information: for example, about training or deployment schedules or how spouses can reach deployed troops
- An advocate: someone to try to get help for you
- Advice or education: people with experience to recommend the best solution for someone in your situation
- Emotional or social support
- Professional counseling
- A helping hand: loans, donations, or services to help out with some of your responsibilities
- Activities: for fitness, recreation, stress relief, or family bonding
- Other needs that do not fit into the categories above (please specify).

If respondents listed more than two types of help needed for any problem, they were asked to choose the top two types of needs for the problem. The goal of this approach was to generate a sense of whether the types of help typically offered reflected the types of help typically desired, independent of specific resources for assistance.

Use of Resources

For each of the respondents' needs, we asked them to indicate which resources, if any, they had "used or tried to use to meet [the] need." The list of resources was the same for all problem domains and needs, and it included the following options for Army and nonmilitary contacts:

Army Contacts

- Army FRG
- Unit members not in the chain of command
- Installation Morale, Welfare, and Recreation (MWR) (for example, recreation or sports services such as intramural sports, libraries, or post gymnasium)
- Army Community Service (ACS) (for example, financial services, relocation assistance, and family services)
- Child and Youth Services (for example, on-post childcare or youth sports)
- Army OneSource, post homepage, or other military Internet resources or social media (such as Twitter or Facebook)
- Chain of command (squad leaders, noncommissioned officers [NCOs] or officers, rear detachment commanders, Sexual Harassment/Assault Response and Prevention advocates, or designated points of contact for family issues)
- Chaplain or members of military religious or spiritual group
- Counselor or doctor provided by the military
- Relief or aid society (Army Emergency Relief [AER])
- Other military contacts (please specify).

Nonmilitary Contacts

- Government or community resources for family services (for example, Temporary Assistance for Needy Families, Special Supplemental Nutrition Program for Women, Infants, and Children, public library, Head Start, or community center)
- Private clubs, organizations, or recreation or fitness centers
- Private, off-post childcare
- Religious or spiritual group or leader
- Private doctor or counselor
- Internet resources (such as WebMD, Google, Craigslist, Wikipedia, Yahoo!, Twitter, or Facebook)
- Personal networks (friends or family)
- Other nonmilitary contacts (please specify).

For each resource a participant indicated that they contacted, they were asked to rate "how well each of these contacts you made helped to meet your needs" for each of their top-two problems. Ratings were made on a scale from 1 = "not at all" to 5 = "very well."

Participants who had used resources were also provided with a list of all the Army resources listed here and asked to rate "what impact, if any, might there be if you were no longer able to access the following resources to help you address any problems you or your family might face." Response options were "Little to no impact on me or my family"; "Some impact on me or my family"; "Serious impact on me or my family"; or "I don't know whether there would be any impact."

Survey Sampling and Procedure

A detailed description of the sampling plan is provided by Sims, Trail, et al. (2017), but in brief, the goal was to obtain responses from a representative sample of active component Army soldiers stationed within the continental United States (CONUS) at Army-led garrisons. We wanted to obtain enough participants to enable statistically acceptable comparisons between subpopulations (e.g., paygrade groups, family status). We used a stratified sample design to draw a representative sample of soldiers, using two levels of stratification. The first level was defined by installation characteristics developed for Installation Management Command called "workforce category," which took into account whether it was a full-service garrison, the population size, and the number of multimission criteria met (U.S. Department of the Army, 2010), as well as other issues (see the 2012 Army MWR Services survey for greater detail; ICF International, 2012a; ICF International, 2012b). The second level of stratification was defined by soldier characteristics and included paygrade (Junior Enlisted: E1–E4; Noncommissioned Officers: E5–E9; Junior Officers: O1–O3; and Senior Officers: O4–O8) and family status (single, married with no children, married with children). Note that our sample pull did not include students or trainees, although we did otherwise oversample junior personnel. Our purpose in excluding these personnel was to make sure we focused on soldiers who had had some time with the freedom to manage their own challenges, rather than soldiers whose primary experience of the Army was in a very structured and time-regimented training environment.

The survey was administered online and was completely anonymous. The survey instrument was available on a nonmilitary website maintained by RAND, and sampled soldiers were sent an initial email and several reminder emails containing a link to the survey. The main sample of 34,250 soldiers received the initial email introducing the project and inviting participation in the survey in late September 2014. The second, supplemental sample of 29,565 soldiers was drawn in early December 2014 and invited to take the survey in December 2014 and early January 2015 (see Sims, Trail, et al., 2017, for additional details about the survey procedure).

Response Rate and Weighting

Just over 7,000 soldiers completed the survey (N = 7,092), for a response rate of 12 percent (see Sims, Trail, et al., 2017, for more information about the response rate). To ensure that the results presented in this report are representative of the demographics of the Army population, we weighted the data using poststratification weighting methods.

Data Analytic Approach

For the present analysis, we examined the number of responses from each garrison represented in the sample and selected the garrisons that had at least 200 unweighted survey responses for further analysis (see Table 2.1 for a list of selected garrisons and number of survey respondents). Garrisons with fewer than 200 responses were not selected because of the loss of statistical power and precision associated with low sample sizes. We set the cutoff at 200 because the nature of the survey—in which respondents select two problem domains, select their needs for those problem domains, and indicate which resources they used to address those needs—divides respondents into

Table 2.1
Garrisons Selected for Analysis and Number of Survey Respondents

Garrison	Number of Survey Respondents
Fort Bragg	246
Fort Campbell	239
Fort Eustis	466
Fort Gordon	447
Fort Hood	241
Fort Huachuca	202
Fort Jackson	347
Fort Knox	254
Fort Leavenworth	658
Fort Meade	264
Fort Polk	231
Fort Rucker	394
Fort Sill	563
Total	**4,552**

smaller and smaller subgroups (e.g., those who had problems with their own well-being versus those who did not; those who contacted a chaplain for help versus those who did not). A respondent size of 200 was estimated to be the minimum number to provide for a variety of garrisons for analysis (13 in total) while maintaining enough respondents to allow for statistical analysis. Although we selected garrisons for further study based on numbers of unweighted respondents to ensure we had enough individuals underlying our analyses to be able to draw more definitive conclusions, we present weighted analyses in this report.

To analyze the survey results by garrison, we reasoned that conducting comparisons between each garrison and all others would require so many statistical tests that the chances of finding a significant difference by chance would be very likely. However, adjusting for the probability of finding a significant result by chance alone (e.g., through a Bonferroni correction) would not be statistically efficient because it would be overly conservative. Another possibility we considered was choosing a reference garrison and making all comparisons to this reference (e.g., comparing all selected garrisons to Fort Hood). We decided against this method for two reasons: (1) there is no clear reference garrison for the Army as a whole regarding issues of problems and needs; and (2) choosing a garrison that fell in the middle of the distribution of scores would require changing the reference garrison for every analysis, which would make the results difficult to interpret.

Thus, we chose to compare all selected garrisons to the *overall average* of all garrisons in the larger sample (i.e., including those with too few unweighted respondents to be selected for more in-depth study). This method required only one omnibus test of a garrison effect (i.e., overall, did garrisons significantly differ from the average), and 13 follow-up comparisons for each significant omnibus effect (i.e., each selected garrison to the overall mean). This method also provided a consistent standard by which each garrison could be judged: the average score across CONUS Army garrisons. However, we would still potentially be conducting a large number of follow-up tests (13 for each significant omnibus garrison effect). Thus, as in Sims, Trail, et al. (2017), to protect against type 1 errors[1] we set the criteria for significance of the omnibus garrison test at alpha equals .05, and the criteria for significance for follow-up comparisons at alpha equals .01.

We analyzed the data by constructing multiple regression models comparing each sampled garrison to the overall average of respondents at all garrisons, including those not selected for comparison. Continuous measures were analyzed using multivariate linear regression models, and binary measures were analyzed using multivariate logistic regression models. Since the analysis of the overall survey results revealed differences

---

[1]   A type 1 error is a statistical test that is found to be significant by chance alone, a possibility when many statistical tests are performed using the same data. We minimized this possibility both by minimizing the number of tests and by using more stringent criteria for significance.

by rank and family status, we included these variables as covariates in the current models (see Sims, Trail, et al., 2017, for a full reporting of rank and family status differences in the survey results).

Site Visit Methodology

We selected garrisons for site visits from the subset of garrisons that had more than 200 unweighted survey responses (Table 2.1). Garrisons were chosen based on the number and type of problems, needs, and resources used at each garrison, and the percentage of soldiers at the garrison with unmet needs.[2] That is, we based our selection largely on responses to the survey rather than on other observable garrison characteristics, although we did purposefully include a range of rural and urban locations, as this was thought to affect availability of non-Army resources. Based on these selection criteria, the four garrisons selected for site visits represented four "profiles" on the survey:

1. Typical profile—few differences from average scores on survey variables (Fort Gordon, Georgia)
2. High problems in some areas and high unmet need (Fort Hood, Texas)
3. Relatively low problems, low unmet needs (Fort Huachuca, Arizona)
4. High problems in some areas with high resource use (Fort Meade, Maryland).

As already described, these installations were chosen based on survey responses, and they are notable in several ways in comparison to other Army garrisons. Fort Gordon is home to the U.S. Army Cyber Center of Excellence and also serves as a training location for technical communications skills. It is located next to the small city of Augusta, Georgia. Fort Hood is the largest active-duty armored post in the United States, and it has a large permanent soldier population. Given this large soldier population and Fort Hood's status as home of III Corps, of the four installations we visited, Fort Hood was the one whose soldiers were most likely to deploy. It is located in central Texas near the small town of Killeen, and about an hour and a half away from the state capital of Austin. Fort Huachuca is home of the U.S. Army Intelligence Center and School, and it is located in a relatively rural location, next to the town of Sierra Vista, Arizona, close to the Mexican border, and more than an hour away from Tucson. Fort Meade has a relatively small Army population for the size of the installation and a large National Security Administration campus. It is located in a large urban area, the National Capitol Region between Baltimore and Washington, D.C., and is near Walter Reed National Military Medical Center, as well as other military

---

[2] "Unmet needs" does not mean an absence of problems, or needs. Rather, we defined someone as having unmet needs if all resources used in attempting to address a given problem and need were rated as meeting the need less than "well."

medicine resources. The missions and duties of soldiers stationed at Forts Gordon, Huachuca, and Meade make gaining and retaining appropriate security clearances of paramount importance for soldiers. At the time of our interviews, Forts Gordon and Meade were the only Army installations growing. None of these installations could be said to be reflective of the Army average, if there is such a thing; all were unique in some way. However, the focus groups and interviews conducted at these locations served to bring further depth and color to the survey analyses.

All four installations had soldiers and families experiencing challenges in their Army lives, and each provided a variety of services and programs to assist them to meet those challenges. These included ACS, which brings together under one umbrella a variety of resources ranging from financial counseling to guidance on caring for infants; medical services, ranging from relatively small clinics to hospitals; barracks and family lodging and assistance; and uniformed chaplain resources to provide confidential spiritual guidance. The communities surrounding the installations provided various resources as well, including military and, in some cases, civilian medical care to which soldiers might be referred, as well as recreation and leisure resources including Texas hill country natural reserves for hiking and outdoor activities and other entertainment options, and businesses that are eager to include soldiers and their families in their customer base.[3] Collecting qualitative data gave us a chance to examine how some of the unique circumstances of installations, as well as commonalities of Army life, affect our findings.

RAND research teams visited selected installations between April and June 2016. During site visits, we conducted focus groups with soldiers (across rank groups), spouses, and service providers.[4] When key service providers could not attend a focus group, we conducted individual interviews with them. Further description of the focus group protocol appears in the next section; interviews with service providers followed the same protocol as the service provider focus groups. Participant characteristics at each location are shown in Table 2.2. The total number of people in the focus groups and interviews was 320.

Description of Focus Group Protocol

Given our desire to incorporate the perspective of junior soldiers in particular, we went through Army channels to make sure that participants had permission from their commanders to attend the sessions. Thus, we worked with a local point of contact, who in turn worked with the post units to identify soldiers and service providers who could be

---

[3]   Readers interested in additional work regarding installations and their surrounding communities may wish to consult Meadows et al., 2013; Meadows, Miller, and Miles, 2014; and Lachman, Resetar, and Camm, 2016.

[4]   Although the initial survey had been administered only to soldiers, the RAND team expanded its scope for the in-person discussions and designed focus groups to include a broad set of stakeholders at each of the four installations (e.g., service providers and spouses).

Table 2.2
Interviews and Focus Groups

	Installations				
	Meade	Hood	Huachuca	Gordon	Total
Interviews	1	1	3	4	**9**
Focus groups	13	12	12	12	**49**
Focus groups with soldiers	9	7	8	8	**32**
Focus groups with spouses and FRGs	2	3	2	2	9
Focus groups with service providers	2	2	2	2	8
Junior and midlevel soldiers (E1–E5)	2	14[a]	16	19	51
NCOs (E6–E9)	15	15	22	18	70
Officers (incl. both 01-03 and 04-05, company- and field-grade officers)	21	19	37	26	103
Soldier participants in focus groups	38	48	75	63	224
By Family Status[b]					
Single	22	20	44	33	119
With spouse or partner	16	28	31	30	105
No kids	22	26	59	44	151
With kids	16	22	16	19	73
By Affiliation					
Spouse participants in focus groups	9	3	9	9	30
Service provider participants in focus groups	17	12	16	21	66

NOTES: [a]This number (14) reflects the total number of soldiers participating in Fort Hood Focus Group 1 ("Single Soldiers from Various Units") and Focus Group 2 ("Married Soldiers from Various Units"). All 14 of these open-paygrade focus group participants have been counted as "junior soldiers," though some are likely to have come from other paygrades. As such, these figures should be viewed as approximations.

[b]Due to logistical challenges (e.g., participants arriving late) and the potential that participants were reluctant to disclose this information in a group setting and at the outset of the focus group, the total number of soldiers with a spouse or partner and/or child is likely to be higher than what is shown in the table.

made available for focus groups. We asked for these soldiers to be separated in terms of paygrade groups and to be diverse with respect to family status but otherwise representative of the unit.[5] We recruited fewer junior soldiers than we anticipated (especially at Fort Meade), so focus group results for junior soldiers should be interpreted with caution. Service providers were generally divided into two groups, one group made up of mental and behavioral health-related providers (including chaplains), and another, more general group that included providers for child services, morale, recreation, and leisure, as well as ACS. When working with our local points of contact, we requested that they recruit participants who were diverse with regard to the characteristics of interest in our study (e.g., family status). However, we did not control participant recruitment, so it is reasonable to characterize participants as a convenience sample, particularly the spouses.

At the start of each focus group, we introduced members of the research team and briefly described the project's focus and the goal of our site visit. We asked soldiers if they were interested in participating and gained their informed consent before proceeding further. When describing the survey research that was the first step in our study, we distributed sheets with the "problem" categories from the survey with illustrative examples. During the introduction to the focus group, we took an informal poll of respondents, asking, by show of hands, who was married, had children, lived on post, etc., and then asking respondents to go around the room and state how long they had been at the installation.

One researcher facilitated the group discussion, with another researcher listening and sometimes asking follow-up questions. We asked permission of participants to tape-record the session, with the additional request that they not use names or other identifiable information while we were recording. A research assistant took detailed notes during the discussion.

All facilitators used the same discussion guide (see the Appendix) as a basis for their questions, which helped maintain consistency regarding the general topics covered across focus groups. The discussion guide started with questions on what respondents felt were the most common problems facing soldiers and their families at the garrison. Subsequent prompts focused on how soldiers get information about resources, the quality of resources on post, and perceived barriers to and facilitators of resource use. Similar protocols were used to question spouses and service providers, with adjustments made to reflect differing participant perspectives on the questions. For example, service providers were asked what they saw as the most common problems facing soldiers and families, particularly among the soldiers they served. Thus, the focus of our study was squarely on the perceived challenges of soldiers and their families, and how those were addressed.

---

[5] Note that neither we nor, indeed, our local point of contact had any way to definitively ensure that this was the case.

Data Analysis Procedures

We analyzed the detailed notes of the focus groups using Dedoose qualitative analysis software.[6] First, notes of the focus groups were cleaned and reviewed by note takers. When necessary, for example, when the conversation moved very quickly or the note taker was not able to capture multiple points of view, the notes were verified against audio recordings of the focus groups or interviews. Notes files were then loaded into Dedoose. An initial coding scheme was developed in consultation with all researchers involved in site visits. It drew on the discussion guide, which in some ways mirrored the survey domains but was expanded to include common themes or topics that emerged in focus groups and interviews. Three members of the research team, all of whom participated in the site visits, applied codes to interview and focus group notes. This initial codebook was extended and refined during the coding process; the coding team met frequently to discuss discrepancies or ambiguities among categories or in the source materials.

When developing the coding scheme, we took into account all detailed notes, without regard to respondent group characteristics, installation, etc. After the coding scheme was finalized and applied to all notes, we then analyzed the representation of the different installations and paygrade groups within each theme, in order to discern if some themes were more common among certain sites or respondent groups. Our review of the coding results (themes by respondent characteristics) focused on (1) ensuring that any leading themes we identified were in fact broadly reported across multiple focus groups and multiple installations, and (2) identifying any trends in which themes were overrepresented in a paygrade group or at a specific installation. We did not have a standard threshold for making either determination; rather, we took a conservative approach to declaring crosscutting themes (or group- or installation-specific themes) through a consensus discussion process involving all coders and site visit personnel.

Focus group results from the spouse focus groups are explicitly noted in the report, as are the results of the service provider focus groups and interviews. Where not noted, the responses were from soldier focus groups.

Strengths and Limitations of Methods

All research methods are subject to limitations of one form or another. By using a mixed-methods approach incorporating both quantitative and qualitative components, we could contravene some issues associated with each approach and benefit from the complementarity of both. A quantitative approach such as a survey offers the opportunity to collect information from a large number of respondents and, owing to the

---

[6] Dedoose is a web application for mixed-methods research.

representativeness of a sample, to be able to speak to averages and trends at the group level that apply to a large number of people. However, because a survey requires that standardized questions be administered (even when fairly tailored branching is used, as in our case), it does not facilitate an in-depth perspective on unique individual experiences. Surveys administered at only one point in time, moreover, offer a snapshot of that time and hence are limited in their ability to portray a process, such as encountering challenges and coping with them, that naturally unfolds over time.

On the other hand, qualitative approaches such as focus groups and interviews offer the opportunity to explore more deeply the experience of the individual, including how a process might unfold over time for them. Focus groups in particular offer a balance between multiple respondents' perspectives so findings are not so overwhelmingly driven by the individual, but they do not provide the same level of individual detail as interviews. Qualitative techniques offer a particular advantage when a content area is not sufficiently developed to generate useful standardized questions, when an inherently process-oriented content area is the object of study and requires detailed information to clarify the mechanics of that process, or when additional detail is necessary to explicate some findings from quantitative methods. However, both approaches, even when used together, have limitations.

The majority of the data presented, both quantitative (survey) and qualitative (focus groups and interviews), reflects individual perceptions. Thus, it is uniquely suited to offer insights into how soldiers and, in some cases, families perceive and cope with the challenges they face, and what resources they perceive are available. While we did speak to service providers at each location, it should be noted that the focus of this study was on the soldier and family experience. Thus, we spoke to service providers about their perspectives on soldier and family problems and how they tried to address them. In some cases, soldiers discussed challenges, and service providers' perspectives echoed soldiers' perspectives. In other cases, service providers were able to speak to a broader context and efforts to address their perceptions of soldier and family needs. However, the information here speaks to one part of the context that is required for determining solutions to challenges that in many cases may be ongoing.

With regard to the survey used in this study, the data analysis was limited to garrisons with enough responses to support analysis, and therefore do not represent the Army as a whole. The initial survey itself was purposely limited to examining CONUS installations, and despite robust attempts to generate participation, at some locations relatively few respondents answered our survey questions. However, although the number of respondents is in some cases smaller than preferred, we were able to explore local differences and provide reliable estimates at a variety of installations in terms of both mission set and location.

We also wish to note some specific limitations of the qualitative methods (focus groups and interviews) used in this study. First, we spoke with soldiers and family members about problems and resource use during focus groups. However, some individual and family problems, such as substance abuse, interpersonal violence, infidelity, and mental health issues, may be less likely to be raised during focus group discussions due to social desirability bias or concerns about privacy or confidentiality. We took several steps to mitigate these types of challenges. For example, we did not restrict soldiers to speaking of only their own experiences but instead purposefully requested that they speak of soldiers generally, or soldiers in their command. Not only would this assist in providing somewhat greater generalizability and a better overview of problems, needs, and resource use than what might be generated by speaking only to individual experiences, but it also supported the reporting of stigmatized problems or resource use in a more anonymous way. It is worthwhile to note that we did indeed observe a wide range of problem types and resource use, which suggests that our approach succeeded in its aims.

Second, because focus group respondents were recruited by local contacts and because participation was voluntary, respondents who participated in focus groups were not necessarily representative of Army soldiers and families at each installation. For example, some respondents mentioned being selected to participate by their unit because they had strong opinions about Army resources or were strong advocates of particular programs, while particularly busy units may not have sent people to participate. In addition, we requested a range of demographic characteristics generally and characteristics such as family status specifically, and our tally of respondent characteristics reflects a considerable amount of diversity on these characteristics.

Third, the installations that we selected to receive site visits were drawn from those that had enough survey respondents to do targeted analysis, which constrained our ability to sample installations that were reflective of Army CONUS installations. However, this approach offered the benefit of being able to compare survey results and findings with focus group results and findings.

Thus, overall, despite these caveats, we judge that our approach achieved the aims of balancing quantitative advantages with qualitative ones and explored more deeply the questions generated by the Army-wide survey analysis. Moreover, we think the mixed-methods approach provides a set of useful and interesting findings. We turn to these findings in the next chapter.

CHAPTER THREE

Results

In this chapter, we report on findings from both the soldier needs survey and the focus groups and interviews. For a number of issues and ranking of top problem domains, we present survey results by garrison. For problems, we show survey results pertaining to the problem areas and focus group respondents' descriptions of the problem within the same section. Other sections discuss survey and focus group results separately and synthesize the mixed-methods results (where applicable).

Survey results illuminate areas where garrisons differ statistically from the "average garrison" as defined by our survey responses, weighted to represent the CONUS Army garrisons. These results highlight areas where a given installation stands out as unusual in terms of challenges faced by soldiers or their process for coping with challenges: the needs that they perceive related to those challenges, patterns of resource use that may be particularly pertinent for a given location's local context, and the ability of local resources to meet their needs. Results that reveal areas where no installations differ from the "average garrison" suggest that local context is not significantly associated with soldier problems or coping processes. Focus group and interview findings (referred to generally as "focus group findings" for ease of reading), on the other hand, offer insight into the way that soldiers, spouses, and service providers see challenges faced by soldiers and the process that they use to address the needs for help generated by those challenges.

The results from these two methods of inquiry are complementary rather than equivalent: the survey results speak to population-level averages at different garrisons versus the Army as a whole, and the focus group results speak to the rich, detailed experiences of focus group participants at each garrison, which may or may not represent the experiences of the population. Thus, the topics that elicited many comments at a garrison are not always reflected in garrison-level differences in the survey data, and vice versa.

Survey Findings for Number of Issues and Top Problem Domains

As detailed by Sims, Trail, et al. (2017),[1] respondents viewed a list of 83 issues within nine problem domains and were instructed to select all the issues they had experienced in the past year. The most frequently selected issues overall were feeling stressed, overwhelmed, or tired; experiencing trouble sleeping; having poor communication with coworkers or superiors; having trouble finding time for sleep, the maintenance of a healthy diet, or physical exercise; experiencing mood changes; having difficulty with long work hours or an inconvenient schedule; and encountering a lack of proper guidance or sponsorship.

As shown in Table 3.1, these were also the top issues within many of the garrisons studied, with some notable exceptions. For example, "rumors or gossip in the military community" was one of the five most selected issues by soldiers at Fort Bragg and Fort Rucker. Similarly, "getting access to military health care (e.g., waiting time for an appointment, distance to treatment facility, availability of needed services, hours or days open)" was one of the five most selected issues by soldiers at Fort Huachuca, Fort Jackson, Fort Knox, and Fort Meade. In addition, "loneliness or boredom" was one of the five most selected issues at Fort Meade and Fort Polk. In addition to loneliness or boredom, "finding nearby or affordable options for recreation, stress relief, or family time" and "not being able to stay at or go to the military installation you prefer" were unique issues commonly selected by soldiers at Fort Polk.

Number of Issues by Garrison

Overall, respondents selected 11.9 issues across all problem domains. As discussed in the data analytic approach section of Chapter Two, we first tested whether the 13 selected garrisons as a whole significantly differed from the overall average (i.e., an omnibus test of garrison differences from average). If this test was statistically significant, we conducted follow-up comparisons to test which of the 13 selected garrisons significantly differed from the overall average. All regressions controlled for paygrade and family status. For number of issues, the 13 selected garrisons as a whole did not significantly differ from the overall average number of issues selected by respondents, $F(13, 7016) = 0.81$, $p = .65$. This suggests that, although soldiers at garrisons each have their own array of challenges, no particular garrison location exacerbates the challenges of daily life in terms of the overall number of issues reported by soldiers over the past year.

Top-Two Problem Domains by Garrison

Respondents next selected the two issues within problem domains that were "the most significant types of problems" they had dealt with in the past year (Sims, Trail, et al., 2017). Overall, the problem domains chosen as soldiers' top problem areas were Military

---

[1]   Sims, Trail, et al. (2017) offers a more in-depth description of the survey, its genesis, and the analyses of overall results for the Army. Rather than repetitively cite it in each new section, we suggest the interested reader consult that document for details on specific items, methods, and approaches.

Table 3.1
Soldiers' Five Most Selected Issues by Garrison and Percentage of Garrison Respondents Selecting Each Issue

Problem Domain	Respondents' Five Most Selected Issues	Bragg	Campbell	Eustis	Gordon	Hood	Huachuca	Jackson	Knox	Leaven-worth	Meade	Polk	Rucker	Sill
Own Well-Being	Feeling stressed, overwhelmed, or tired	52	39	43	47	58	42	47	49	42	40	44	42	51
Military Practices and Culture	Poor communication with coworkers or superiors	47	51	45	44	56	31	42	52	36	49	40	39	45
Own Well-Being	Trouble sleeping	50		37	38	60	34	44		43	47	40	41	52
Work-Life Balance	Finding time for sleep, maintenance of a healthy diet, or physical exercise			37	41	52	30	48		38			37	41
Health Care System	Getting access to military health care (e.g., appointment waiting time, distance to treatment facility, availability of services, hours or days open)						29	42	37		45			
Military Practices and Culture	Lack of proper guidance or sponsorship	53	40		36									
Work-Life Balance	Long work hours or an inconvenient schedule for you		37	39						37				
Military Practices and Culture	Rumors or gossip in the military community	43											37	
Own Well-Being	Loneliness or boredom										42	40		
Military Practices and Culture	Not being able to stay at or go to the military installation you prefer											38		
Own Well-Being	Physical injury or illness													39
Work-Life Balance	Being able to pursue educational opportunities					51								
Military Practices and Culture	Figuring out how to use "the system"—where to go, with whom to talk		35											
Work-Life Balance	Finding nearby or affordable options for recreation, stress relief, or family time											41		
Household Management	Finding suitable housing or encountering poor housing or barracks quality								35					
Military Practices and Culture	Getting people in your unit to listen to you, take you seriously, or treat you with respect								35					

NOTE: All survey respondents were soldiers (N = 7,092).

Table 3.2
The Three Most Cited Problem Domains by Respondents at Each Garrison (%)

	Military Practices and Culture	Work-Life Balance	Soldier's Well-Being	Financial or Legal	Household Management	Health Care System
Bragg	56	25	35			
Campbell	50	35	26			
Eustis	38	24	28			
Gordon	45	24	31			
Hood	53	48	35			
Huachuca	32	29	40			
Jackson	34	33	26			
Knox	23			28		24
Leavenworth	34	30	29			
Meade	43		39			32
Polk	34	41			36	
Rucker	47	25	26			
Sill	32	28	39			

NOTE: All survey respondents were soldiers (N = 7,092). Percentages are for respondents within garrisons. Respondents could choose up to two top problem areas, so percentages may total more than 100 percent.

Practices and Culture, Work-Life Balance, Soldier's Well-Being, Health Care System Problems, and Relationship Problems.

Looking at the three most cited problem domains by garrison, respondents at most garrisons reported the same top problems. As shown in Table 3.2, Military Practices and Culture, Work-Life Balance, and Soldier's Well-Being were the most cited problem domains for 10 of the 13 garrisons. Exceptions were Knox, Meade, and Polk, which all cited Military Practices and Culture as a top problem domain but differed on the other two top problems.

Focus Group, Interview, and Survey Results by Problem Domain

We next analyzed both focus group[2] results and the survey data on soldiers' top problem domains. The purpose of this analysis is to provide greater depth and context to

---

2   Because the large majority of our qualitative data collection was done with focus groups and results were analyzed as a whole, we refer to the findings of the focus groups and individual and small-group interviews collectively as "focus group findings."

Sims, Trail, et al.'s (2017) findings on soldiers' problems and their coping strategies for dealing with them. For each problem domain, we first detail findings from the focus groups, then discuss significant variations across garrisons in the problem domain (if any) found in the survey. Finally, we analyze findings from the focus groups to provide explanations for how garrison context affects the problems soldiers and their families face.

Military Practices and Culture
Focus Group Findings
Respondents described several problems that fell within the survey domain of Military Practices and Culture that they felt were leading problems for soldiers and families.

For younger soldiers and families new to the Army, a key issue described by respondents related to their expectations for Army life compared with the reality encountered. While a period of adjustment is expected, experienced soldiers described how there is more distance between contemporary civilian culture and military culture than there used to be. They described how new soldiers do not always acculturate well, especially those who arrive with little respect for authority and precedence, and who are not shy about questioning authority. NCOs expressed the view that new soldiers' lack of willingness to keep their heads down and do the work makes it more difficult to lead.

Respondents described the relationships between chain of command and the soldiers in their command as key to unit cohesion and readiness. However, they also discussed their perception that there **used to be more time for and emphasis on training leaders in how to lead and supporting efforts to build relationships between NCOs and junior soldiers**. In their view, increased time pressures (e.g., a result of high operational tempo, lower leader-to-soldier ratios, and the increased burdens of paperwork and mandatory training) were crowding out the time required for these important tasks. This resulted in a lack of time and resources devoted to developing and training leaders, but respondents also linked the problem to leaders being promoted too quickly or having too many people in their command to be able to be effective managers. As a Fort Hood respondent pointed out, "People get promoted to leader levels but have not developed as leaders, and leadership cannot be passed down." The sponsorship program, which is ostensibly a vehicle to provide mentoring, support, and acculturation for junior soldiers, was described as an unevenly implemented program in the sense that it depended on the quality and experience of the person doing the sponsoring, and **most respondents had low expectations for what sponsors were supposed to do**.

Another aspect of military practices and culture that was cited as a problem for soldiers was changing views on how junior soldiers should be disciplined. Although respondents disagreed about the most effective techniques for exerting authority over soldiers in one's unit (e.g., harsher methods versus winning hearts and minds), many **complained that systems currently in place to discipline soldiers are slow and ineffective** as mechanisms to maintain control within units. There were complaints that paperwork-based processes for disciplining soldiers take so long (e.g., an Article 15—nonjudicial punishment for misconduct—can take a month) that it sends the message to others in the units that soldiers can disobey or disrespect more-senior NCOs and incur no immediate consequences.

Focus groups with Army leaders also revealed problem areas related to contemporary Army structure and processes. **Respondents complained that Army policies focused on hot-topic problems and were reactionary rather than strategic.** The consequence, according to respondents, was too many policies and a climate of over-regulation, including mandatory trainings on topics ranging from suicide prevention to equal opportunity policy to human trafficking. The proliferation of these types of training and requirements (including those related to soldier discipline, as described previously) was cited by focus group respondents as one reason they do not have the time to supervise soldiers and actually train for the mission. Further, as one experienced officer complained, the Army does not provide leaders with a good way to prioritize among so many mandatory activities, and, in his words, "if everything is a priority, then nothing is a priority."

Another problem related to military practices and culture raised by midcareer and more-senior Army leaders was concerns about downsizing. This problem spanned several related issues, including concerns about added work burden when experienced soldiers were being let go and not replaced, a sense that poor-quality junior soldiers were being promoted, and fear and uncertainty around reduced promotion rates for more-senior staff, especially at the field-grade officer level. **Respondents felt that these changes in Army retention policies had fostered a climate in which soldiers felt that they needed to be looking out for their own interests, because the Army would not necessarily be taking care of them** as they had been told or believed it would in years past.

Survey Results

A multivariate logistic regression controlling for paygrade and family status revealed significant garrison differences in respondents' choice of Military Practices and Culture as a top-two problem [Wald $\chi^2(13) = 26.4$, $p = .02$]. As shown in Figure 3.1, respondents at Bragg chose Military Practices and Culture as a top-two problem more frequently than average [54 percent compared with 38 percent; Wald $\chi^2(1) = 6.08$, $p = .01$], with more than half indicating that this was a top challenge they faced in the past year. Garrisons did not significantly differ in the number of Military Practices and Culture issues selected.

Summary of Garrison Context and Problems with Military Practices and Culture

Respondents at different garrisons did not differ on the number of Military Practices and Culture issues they experienced in the past year. However, Bragg respondents were more likely than the "average garrison" respondents to *prioritize* that domain as one of the top two challenges faced in the prior year. Although each garrison context is different, respondents across our site visits described how changes in Army culture and military

Figure 3.1
Garrison Differences in Percentage of Respondents Who Chose Military Practices and Culture as a Top-Two Problem

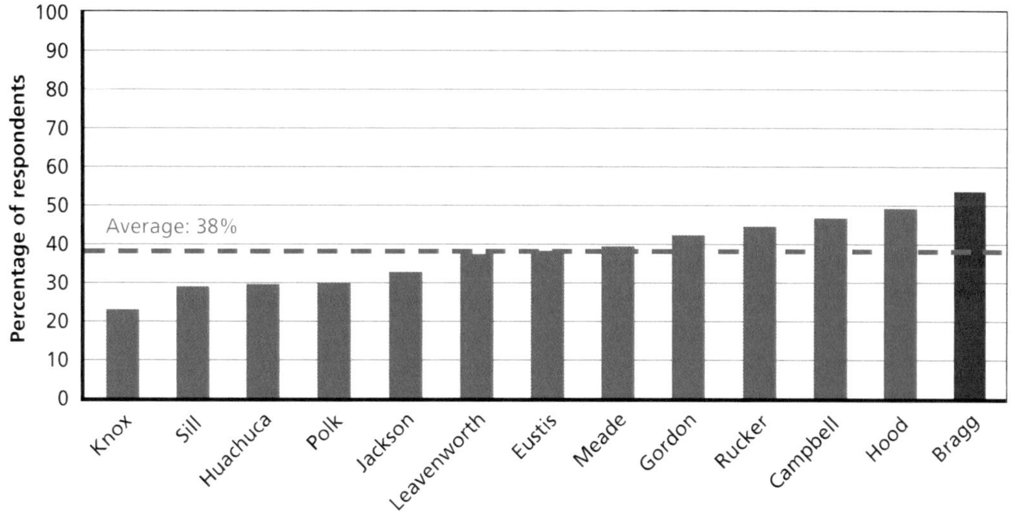

NOTE: All survey respondents were soldiers (N = 7,092). The percentage of respondents who chose Military Practices and Culture as a top-two problem was significantly higher at Fort Bragg compared to the overall Army average (38 percent). All comparisons controlled for paygrade and family status.
RAND *RR2148A-3.1*

practices in general presented problems for soldiers; focus group findings also suggested more similarity across the Army than difference. Given that issues relating to Army systems and administration were included in this domain, this is perhaps unsurprising.

Work-Life Balance
Focus Group Findings

Work-Life Balance was an area of stress and concern for some focus group respondents. Some respondents discussed the challenges of childcare issues, such as dropping kids off at day care and then arriving on time to physical training (PT), or the challenge of arranging care for sick children. **Respondents also discussed the stressful reality of a "24-hour Army,"** where shift work was often required and workloads were high, with the expectation that work would get done even if that meant working long hours (e.g., answering email after work hours). **There was a sense that this burden fell particularly heavily at the midcareer level**, among NCOs and officers who had leadership responsibilities and obligations to support the rest of the chain of command. According to respondents, several factors exacerbated the workload pressure on units, including units having been downsized or not operating at full capacity (e.g., because of soldiers on medical leave or soldiers who were waiting on authorizations to begin work) and the compounding effects of small but frequent taskings for units to contribute to installation needs. These effects were mentioned frequently at Fort Hood, where unit leaders complained that having to send even a few soldiers to support general installation operations (e.g., cutting grass) or special needs (e.g., supporting community events) was a serious drain on the unit's ability to train for its mission. Last, traffic and commuting burdens were reported by some respondents, who might choose to live farther off post for better schools or affordable housing, but who then struggled with substantial delays getting on or off post during peak arrival and departure hours.

Particular groups, such as platoon sergeants and Advanced Individual Training instructors at Training and Doctrine Command posts, seemed to have particularly challenging schedules. Not surprisingly, respondents from units with continuous deployment rotations or working within intensive training cycles also seemed to describe greater work-life balance problems. Parents' work-life balance was affected by childcare issues, especially single parents and dual military couples, though this did not necessarily mean that parents were the only ones facing work-life challenges.

Survey Results

Significant garrison differences in respondents' choice of Work-Life Balance as a top-two problem are shown in Figure 3.2 [Wald $\chi^2(13)$ = 34.8, p < .001]. Respondents at Hood chose Work-Life Balance as a top-two problem more frequently than average [49 percent compared with 31 percent; Wald $\chi^2(1)$ = 7.14, p = .008]. Garrisons did not significantly differ in the number of Work-Life Balance issues selected, suggesting that issues within this domain were fairly consistent in terms of frequency regardless of the location of respondents.

Figure 3.2
Garrison Differences in Percentage of Respondents Who Chose Work-Life Balance as a Top-Two Problem

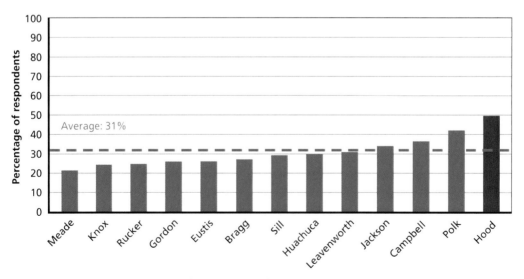

NOTE: All survey respondents were soldiers (N = 7,092). The percentage of respondents who chose Work-Life Balance as a top-two problem was significantly higher at Fort Hood compared to the overall Army average (31 percent). All comparisons controlled for paygrade and family status.
RAND RR2148A-3.2

Summary of Garrison Context and Problems with Work-Life Balance

Among focus groups Work-Life Balance was a concern for some, particularly for cadre and instructors at Training and Doctrine Command posts. About a third of survey respondents cited Work-Life Balance as one of two top problem issues, with Fort Hood soldiers standing out for citing this issue more frequently in surveys. This higher level of concern may stem from the intense training schedules in preparation for deployments cited by focus group respondents at Fort Hood.

Soldier's Well-Being

Focus Group Findings

When soldiers described problems related to their own well-being, they frequently attributed the problems to work-related stress. **Soldier respondents reported work-related stress due to units being short staffed or having too much work put on their units.** Some senior leaders complained about a lack of effective midlevel leaders, which resulted in relatively senior soldiers getting involved in issues that should have been the purview of a lieutenant or a team leader.

Respondents also described how working on operational missions while in garrison can affect soldiers' well-being. Examples of operational missions conducted while in garrison include participating in highly classified intelligence work and providing remote support for operational missions, such as piloting unmanned aircraft. Soldiers and service providers described the challenge of transitioning from high-stakes operational work during the duty day to an in-garrison atmosphere after hours, for example, at the gym or at home with their families. According to participants, the stress of the work and tension between operational and nonoperational environments were causes of or contributors to mental health and relationship issues. Compounding this issue, they reported limited resources to engage in activities that they thought would help relieve this stress. Respondents perceived a lack of activities, places to go off post, and common areas on post as a challenge for soldiers who wanted to unwind and hang out with friends. This seemed to be a problem at Fort Gordon more than other installations we visited. For example, two respondents in different focus groups at Fort Gordon referred to the Warrior Zone at Fort Riley (though note that Fort Riley is a much larger installation) as a recreation space for permanent party soldiers to play video games or watch television together, and complained that Fort Gordon lacked a similar facility. They commented that the barracks were small and crowded, and it was depressing to have nowhere else to go.

However, some leaders and service providers noted a **challenging tendency of many junior soldiers to prefer staying in the barracks**—playing video games, for example, or watching Netflix—rather than showing up for events or engaging in activities. This theme came up for junior soldiers across the installations we visited, but the concern was more pronounced and widely shared by participants at Fort Gordon, who explained this behavior as a personality characteristic that was more common in the type of soldiers who were training there. In a different way, this type of behavior was thought to contribute to soldier well-being problems. For example, service providers also noted feelings of isolation and disconnection as being common for soldiers and Army families. They felt that this was a serious problem that contributed to *but was also partially caused by* problems with chain of command and peer relationships; they described a cycle of soldiers and families being reluctant to engage with the Army community, which prevented them from forming the relationships that would make them feel welcome and supported.

Some soldier and family respondents described how **Army regulations and culture in some ways limited time and opportunities for personal development (e.g., taking college classes or working toward a promotion)** and family responsibilities (e.g., moving[3] or dealing with a family member's illness or death) because soldiers were expected to take care of these things without appropriate leave or on their own time. They noted that this placed stress on soldiers who struggled to meet their personal goals and the needs of their families while remaining in good standing with the Army.

Respondents also observed that **performance expectations were felt more keenly because of the broader context of a shrinking Army.** One respondent described how it is now harder for people to make mistakes without feeling as though their careers will be over, and there was a sense among several respondents that rules or requirements for promotion or expectations for their performance are continually changing, which decreases their sense of control over their career and increases feelings of uncertainty.

Finally, **soldiers sometimes raised issues concerning nutrition and the availability of healthy food**, which our survey classified within the domain of personal well-being. They reported that some soldiers who lived in barracks relied primarily on microwaves to prepare their food, and respondents felt this presented a challenge to healthy eating. There were also complaints that the hours of the dining facility and sometimes long lines during peak meal times made it challenging to eat well on post.

With the exception of the need for common spaces and recreation opportunities being raised more often at Fort Gordon than at other installations, there were no noticeable variations by garrison in the types or frequency of soldier well-being problems reported by respondents. However, respondents described soldier well-being problems—and requests for related services—as largely related to soldiers' work roles, and these problems would therefore be expected to be more common in units with operational responsibilities or where irregular shift work is required, regardless of location.

Survey Results

Garrisons did not significantly differ in the number of Soldier's Well-Being issues selected or the choice of Soldier's Well-Being as a top-two problem.

Summary of Garrison Context and Problems with Soldier's Well-Being

Focus group results suggest that issues with soldier well-being frequently stem from work-related stress, often related to high work demands coupled with unit manning

---

[3]   In some cases moving itself can be seen as a manifestation of Army regulations and culture; we use it here in the sense that it is something that must be accomplished outside duty hours.

shortages. Inadequately experienced leaders contribute to the problem, as do intense work schedules that preclude stress-reduction activities and the lack of off-post activities. The tendency of junior personnel to prefer self-directed activities such as playing video games or watching movies was thought to exacerbate the problem. Other sources of stress affecting well-being included limited time for personal development, concern over high performance expectations, and challenges to being able to eat healthy meals.

Household Management
Focus Group Findings

When asked about leading problems facing soldiers and their families, respondents often raised issues related to housing—including barracks, on-post family housing, and off-post housing—which was captured in the survey category of Household Management. Because many housing-related issues and complaints were specific to one or two installations and thus help illustrate how challenges may differ by post and why a local perspective can be helpful, we describe installation-specific differences in respondents' reports of housing problems throughout the themes here. For example, both Fort Meade and Fort Gordon were growing during our data collection period, and they may have been experiencing some challenges in managing that growth, including in terms of optimal housing assignment and allocation.[4]

Many soldiers living on post shared their dissatisfaction with the quality of housing and the perceived value of on-post housing (compared to off-post housing). Focus group participants described the policy of the Army's privatized housing partners to base the rental amount on a soldier's Basic Allowance for Housing and to assign the size of the housing (number of bedrooms) based on family size alone. This situation resulted in soldiers of different paygrades but similar family size paying substantially different amounts for nearly identical housing, which respondents felt was unfair. This practice was particularly frustrating for soldiers and families living at Fort Meade and Fort Gordon, who noted that off-post housing gave a better value to soldiers, in terms of the amount of space and the quality of the housing that one could rent or buy for the same price as on-post housing. A related issue, raised by only one respondent, was that Army housing assignment limited the number of bedrooms based on family size, preventing families from having an extra bedroom for hosting guests.[5] This respondent described how having space to host out-of-town guests was important to his family and to many Army families because they were often living far

---

[4] OACSIM notes that the Army also has processes in place to collect information on the housing concerns of their communities, in order to support both awareness of issues and ongoing improvement efforts.

[5] OACSIM provided clarification on this point and noted that assignment of housing based on family size is an Army regulation, not the Army privatized housing partners' policy. Soldiers that live on post pay rent based on rank, not family size. This superficially shows that families of varying pay grades pay for the "same" house with different rents. Due to excess inventory, occupancy, and/or market competition, housing partners may also offer concessions to entice residents to live in their communities. Partners built homes to appropriately house soldiers and their direct dependents, not additional bedrooms for hosting guests.

from their relatives, and asking or paying for visiting family to stay in a hotel would be a hardship.

Soldiers also voiced frustration with the on-post housing assignment process, which they noted mixed enlisted soldiers of different ranks and enlisted soldiers and officers in the same housing areas. The colocation of soldiers of different ranks was described as socially challenging. For example, socializing with neighbors could inadvertently be fraternization,[6] and both officers and enlisted soldiers described wanting to be able to relax and feel at ease when at their homes, which was challenging given the cross-rank colocation.[7]

Moreover, some respondents complained that **the housing was poorly maintained, especially at Fort Gordon;** although the issue was raised elsewhere, maintenance issues were not as consistently a theme. Soldiers with families at Fort Gordon expressed grievances with the poor quality of housing and the lack of enforcement of both basic standards of health and safety and Army regulations for on-post housing. Respondents described personal experiences of very long waiting times after submitting maintenance requests for what seemed to be serious maintenance concerns, such as mold remediation and repair of broken or inoperable windows.[8] A few participants also commented on the lack of housing policy enforcement that came with privatized housing. For example, one participant contrasted memories of strict enforcement of things such as yard maintenance and pet policies when the Army managed housing, but lamented that the privatized housing partner staff do nothing to enforce policies (e.g., keeping grass trimmed, limits on numbers of pets, keeping dogs on leash). In his words, "[The] housing contractors basically collect your check and you can do whatever you want with your home." Respondents discussed the need for leaders to advocate for soldiers to help resolve housing issues, in part because of the perception that a soldier's paygrade to some degree dictated the type of treatment he or she would receive from the privatized housing staff. When asked whether problems with privatized housing were consistent with experiences in other places, participants mentioned Fort Riley and Fort Knox as examples of well-run privatized housing, and they generally felt that Fort Gordon was experiencing unique challenges with on-post housing.

---

[6]   See Army fraternization policy in U.S. Army (2014); generally, relationships between officers and enlisted soldiers, or NCOs and junior enlisted, are restricted, as are relationships that put at risk perceived authority and discipline, such as between trainer and trainee. The intent is to prevent adverse impacts on morale and discipline by avoiding perceptions of partiality, preference, or other unfairness.

[7]   Although this was described by multiple participants, this outcome is not the result of deliberate strategy. OACSIM noted that residents are typically housed according to their categories (ranks, family size, etc.). Officers and enlisted living next door to each other are one-off situations and are rare.

[8]   OACSIM notes that local inventory mix of older and newer homes may lead to a view that the older homes are not maintained well in comparison to the newer homes. Each location also faces local challenges, which at Fort Gordon include a humid climate that can make facilities more susceptible to maintenance issues such as mold.

A third strand of housing-related problems raised by respondents was related to barracks housing for single soldiers. The majority of soldiers at Fort Huachuca spoke highly of barracks housing, but soldiers at Fort Meade, Fort Gordon, and Fort Hood described quality-of-life concerns, such as some barracks being overcrowded, having inadequate storage space, and providing little to no privacy, since two soldiers often share an open room. Respondents also noted that some of the barracks' living spaces at these installations lacked adequate kitchen facilities to prepare healthy meals. For example, many barracks' kitchens lacked stoves and disallowed hot plates, so resident soldiers who did not have meal cards (e.g., shift workers) depended on microwaves to cook food, which contributed to poor diet choices. Finally, some units' soldiers were spread out across different barracks, which was the source of several problems. At Fort Gordon, because of the prevalence of shift work, soldiers from different units (i.e., some who work shift and others who do not) sharing quarters posed a challenge to all parties' ability to sleep or otherwise use their space as it made sense for their work schedules. NCOs also said that because companies are still responsible for their units, breaking up the units across different barracks has an effect on command and control, in that leaders are forced to monitor soldiers across several different barracks areas. Relationships within units and between unit members and chain of command were also thought to be hurt when units are not colocated in barracks.[9]

A final theme of housing-related problems was that the quality of schools was a major factor for many Army families in choosing where to live. Many respondents stated that they chose to live far from the installation—and tolerate a longer commute—to live in a better-resourced or better-performing public school district. Some respondents recounted giving or being given the advice to live off post or away from certain areas to be within the attendance zone of better schools than were available on or near the installation.

Survey Results

Significant garrison effects emerged for a number of Household Management issues [$F(13, 7010) = 2.28$, $p = .005$]. As shown in Figure 3.3, for the number of Household Management issues selected, controlling for paygrade and family status, Huachuca respondents selected fewer issues than average [mean = 0.95 vs. 1.3, $t(7010) = -4.07$, $p < .001$]. Note that the overall average number of Household Management issues selected was also relatively low (1.3 issues out of 9.0 potential issues).

In addition, significant garrison differences emerged for respondents' choice of Household Management as a top-two problem [Wald $\chi^2(13) = 28.5$, $p = .008$]. As shown in Figure 3.4, respondents at Bragg chose Household Management as a top-two

---

[9] OACSIM notes that many factors may affect barracks assignments, including unit integrity, minimum space/adequacy standard per AR 420-1, and that the quality and conditions of individual barracks rooms can also affect the quantity of assignable barracks spaces.

Figure 3.3
Garrison Difference from Mean Number of Household Management Issues

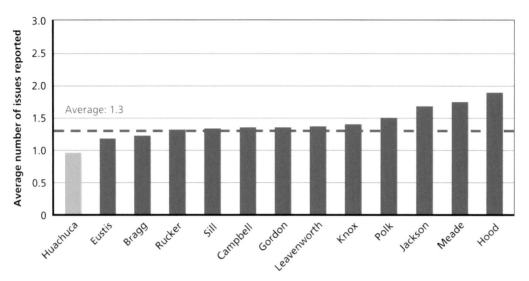

NOTE: All survey respondents were soldiers (N = 7,092). The mean number of Household Management issues was significantly lower at Fort Huachuca compared to the overall Army average (1.3). All comparisons controlled for paygrade and family status.

RAND RR2148A-3.3

Figure 3.4
Garrison Differences in Percentage of Respondents Who Chose Household Management as a Top-Two Problem

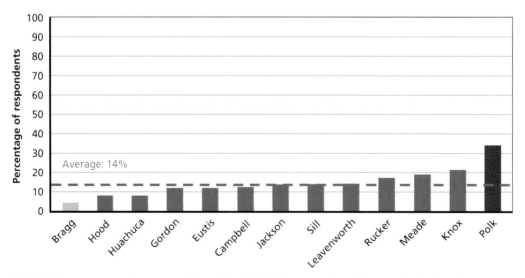

NOTE: All survey respondents were soldiers (N = 7,092). The percentage of respondents who chose Household Management as a top-two problem was significantly higher at Fort Polk compared to the overall Army average (14 percent). All comparisons controlled for paygrade and family status.

RAND RR2148A-3.4

problem less frequently than average [4 percent compared with 14 percent; Wald $\chi^2(1) = 8.25$, $p = .004$], and respondents at Polk chose Household Management as a top-two problem more frequently than average [34 percent; Wald $\chi^2(1) = 12.55$, $p < .001$].

Summary of Garrison Context and Problems with Household Management

The age, quality, and quantity of on-post housing and barracks vary by installation; therefore, the garrison context has a strong relationship to the types of housing problems that soldiers and their families will experience. This was evident in the survey analyses, in which Huachuca respondents listed fewer household management issues overall, while Polk respondents were more likely to choose household management as a top problem and Bragg respondents were less likely to choose it as a top problem.

Focus group results added additional depth to the nature and extent of housing issues experienced by soldiers and their families. One specific aspect of the garrison context raised by the focus group participants was the quality of management or oversight of on-post housing by the privatized housing contractor. Another pertained to housing policies that could lead soldiers to perceive themselves as paying substantially different amounts for identical housing. Single soldiers discussed barracks housing in terms of overcrowding, inadequate kitchens, and policies that did not take unit assignment into account.

Other important contextual factors that vary by garrison and will, according to our focus group respondents, affect housing issues are the cost of housing in the area around the installation and the quality of on-post schools. These factors were mentioned as part of the calculation of whether on-post housing was a reasonable option for soldiers and their families.

Financial or Legal Problems

Focus Group Findings

Few soldiers mentioned experiencing legal issues in the focus groups. Rather, financial challenges drove these discussions. **Participants in the focus groups reported financial issues as a top problem that they saw facing Army soldiers.** Many participants described a pattern of junior soldiers, most of whom lacked basic budgeting skills, "getting in over their heads" by buying things or in other ways living beyond their means. Participants cited purchasing new cars, sometimes with unfavorable interest rates; "blowing" income tax returns and bonuses; and using check cashing services and pawnshops.

In addition to poor personal choices in spending or lack of experience managing money, respondents also reported that administrative errors related to pay or Basic Allowances for Housing were the basis of some soldiers' financial troubles, such as when they unwittingly received too much pay or Basic Allowance for Subsistence while receiving a meal card and then had their pay withheld entirely ("no pay due") until the overpayment was corrected. Respondents at Fort Meade mentioned the high cost of living in that area as increasing soldiers' likelihood of experiencing financial problems. Other types of financial problems related to variation in cost of living between duty locations (e.g., moving to a higher cost-of-living market requires adjustments to a family's budget, despite relative changes in the Basic Allowance for Housing), family emergencies that caused unexpected expenses, and soldiers who came into the Army with preexisting financial issues.

In discussing the types of financial problems faced by soldiers and their families, respondents mentioned several complicating factors that unintentionally fostered them. One NCO lamented that not enough time was devoted to mentoring junior soldiers in order to build the type of trust and have the close involvement that would allow for advice to be given (e.g., go to AER instead of a payday lender) or problems to be detected early. Several respondents stated that financial problems often start small but can quickly get out of control, due in part to junior soldiers' desire for autonomy and reluctance to bring their problems to their leadership.

Financial problems were described as more common among junior enlisted soldiers; for many, the Army is their first experience with receiving a substantial paycheck that they have to manage on their own. However, financial problems were not exclusive to new soldiers; NCOs in particular described seeing financial problems within their peer group.

Respondents mentioned ACS budgeting and financial literacy classes as possible resources to turn to in response to financial problems. AER was also praised as an effective recourse when soldiers are in a financial bind, and many respondents gave examples of how AER helped soldiers in their units with unexpected expenses. However, respondents were also measured in their responses regarding the degree to which a prevention strategy would be an effective approach to soldiers' financial problems. One factor respondents identified that may keep soldiers from disclosing financial problems, beyond a desire for privacy, was a fear of losing security clearance. Consequently, a few respondents and several service providers discussed how financial problems were less likely to be disclosed—and help sought out—by soldiers whose job functions were contingent on their security clearances.

Survey Results

Garrisons did not significantly differ in the number of financial or legal issues selected or the choice of Financial or Legal Problems as a top-two problem.

Summary of Garrison Context and Financial or Legal Problems

Financial and legal problems were discussed equally among the four installations in our site visits. Concerns about financial problems' effects on security clearances would be expected to be concentrated in units or installations where Military Occupational Specialties require clearances. Inadequate time to mentor junior soldiers and build relationships that might head off financial problems was also cited as a contributing factor. Additionally, areas with a higher cost of living could trigger financial issues for new arrivals.

Health Care System Problems
Focus Group Findings

Respondents were quick to point to the health care system as a leading source of problems for soldiers and families, and many respondents shared stories of personal challenges when dealing with the Army health care system. Issues included access to care, experience of care, and, to a lesser extent, complaints about the quality of care received.

Some soldiers expressed frustration about long wait times to see their primary care manager, to receive appropriate referrals, and to get an appointment with an on-post specialist. An officer from Fort Hood summarized the situation: "In terms of health care, it's hard to get an appointment to see a primary care manager. It's about a one month wait time to get a two-minute consultation, and that consult leads to referral, [and it] takes another month to get your appointment with the referral doctor." Some soldiers noted their inability to keep appointments reliably. They needed to schedule appointments several weeks in advance (e.g., for a specialist) because of an unpredictable work schedule. Having to cancel and reschedule appointments was unavoidable, but it caused additional delays.

When experiencing illness or injury, some soldiers described the process of "sick call" (in the installations that had traditional sick call—where a location or clinic has set hours, typically in the morning, during which soldiers with acute issues can go to be seen and referred as needed) as overcrowded, trying, and ineffective. At some installations, when medical facilities were overloaded, soldiers were instructed to go to private, off-post urgent care providers (e.g., Patient First) or to an off-post hospital emergency room, from which significant out-of-pocket costs, copayments, wait times, and coordination of follow-up with Army medical care often resulted. Soldiers who worked within the sanctioned channels of going through sick call and then to their troop medical center first complained that the process was time consuming and that many who present with illness or injury are screened out before seeing a provider (e.g., assessed as likely to recover on their own without medical attention). Related to this process, a few respondents discussed privacy concerns with having to work through so many levels of vetting and triage before having access to a physician's assistant or their primary care manager.

Some respondents criticized the quality of military health care, but others were supportive of the providers, saying that once a patient got in the room with the provider, the care was very good. Several respondents believed that the system was just overburdened with too many patients and too few providers, and that this lack of capacity was at the root of the long wait times. However, some respondents also distinguished between military and civilian medical personnel. Those that did generally suggested that civilian personnel were less competent, less committed, and only working for the Army until something better came along. In a similar vein, some respondents complained about what they perceived to be poor continuity of care and high turnover (not necessarily solely Permanent Change of Station–related) among medical personnel, both of which are consistent with respondents' impressions that Army health care systems may not be a top choice for providers.

A few soldiers complained about a lack of continuity and basic coordination of health care between duty stations for them and their families, with records and prescriptions taking weeks or more to be transferred. One soldier with a spouse in the Exceptional Family Member Program described the experience of starting over at each new installation with the process of establishing a trusted care team and support network within that installation's health care resources. Additionally, there were complaints about TRICARE customer service (and largely automated phone system) and the challenges of using TRICARE benefits to access outside providers and specialists.

Notably, in addition to the problem of undertreated or recurrent health problems as a result of delays and hassles interfacing with the health care system, **a large number of respondents linked health care system problems to the challenge of soldiers taking time away from work to deal with their medical problems.** This theme related most often to perceived inefficiency. For example, a respondent at Fort Meade reported missing half of the workday to drive 45 minutes from Fort Meade to Walter Reed National Military Medical Center in Bethesda, Maryland, and then 1 hour and 45 minutes on the return trip due to traffic, just to have a 5-minute follow-up appointment with a doctor. When complaining about sick call, going to the emergency room, and in some cases waiting at the pharmacy, respondents often noted the extended wait times with disgust. In practice, this time to deal with the health system not only was a "waste" of their time but took significant time away from work, and they either needed to make up that time or members of their unit had to take over their responsibilities.

The theme of taking time away from work to interface with the health care system related to the problem of malingering as well. This refers to soldiers without legitimate medical issues making health care appointments either to get time away from work or PT or to get medically retired based on health problems (and documentation of same). Respondents complained not only that this inappropriate use of the health care system contributed to the long wait times but also that soldiers seeking medical care or being medically excused from work placed a strain on units, in which "every day, soldiers are pulling the weight for the others that are missing." There was widespread agreement among focus group participants that some people were just faking symptoms. However, many respondents also complained about being met with skepticism from medical personnel when they reported pain or overuse injuries and felt that they at times had been disbelieved and needed to "prove" the legitimacy of their illness or injury.

Across installations, focus group respondents disagreed about whether these types of concerns (e.g., wait times and quality of care) were unique to their particular installation. Some soldiers insisted that their current duty station was worse than previous posts, while others believed that these issues are par for the course for Army medical care.

In the focus groups, we did identify some differences in the types of health care system problems raised at the different installations. First, health care system problems seemed to be raised somewhat more frequently at Fort Hood and Fort Meade than at Fort Huachuca and Fort Gordon, with the characteristics of each installation playing into the types of issues noted. At Fort Hood, and to some extent at Fort Huachuca, there were complaints about delays for soldiers who needed physicals or vision and hearing exams to deploy or otherwise perform their duties. This makes sense considering the relative focus on deployability at Fort Hood and some of the duties at Fort Huachuca (e.g., piloting unmanned aerial vehicles). At Fort Meade, the most common grievances were about the proximity—in terms of distance and driving time, taking traffic into account—of medical care facilities that soldiers and their families needed to go to for specialty appointments in particular (e.g., Walter Reed National Military Medical Center). Soldiers and families at Fort Huachuca faced similar challenges, receiving referrals to specialists in Tucson—about a 1.5-hour drive away—or more distant cities. While at Fort Meade, we learned that some soldiers are stationed there as part of a "compassionate reassignment," an accommodation sometimes made for soldiers who are experiencing extreme family problems, such as a serious illness, because of the availability of medical resources in the region—although the primary resources require some travel to reach (particularly in light of Washington, D.C., metro traffic congestion). We also heard that some soldiers saw Fort Meade as a relatively undemanding post, an assignment that they might have received as a respite after spending extended time at locations with a more intense deployment demand. Accordingly, we heard from several soldiers that they have taken time to avail themselves of the medical services offered at Fort Meade and surrounding installations. Because the number of soldiers who are stationed at Fort Meade as a compassionate assignment is likely quite small, we doubt that this phenomenon is driving the difference in health care system problems identified in the survey. However, taken together with the issue of soldiers who may be "catching up" on deferred health care, and given the challenges reported about traveling to and interfacing with multiple health care facilities, the survey finding that Fort Meade has significantly higher rates of health care system problems than other installations is not in conflict with what we heard in the focus groups.

Survey Results

Garrison differences in respondents' choice of Health Care System Problems as a top-two problem are shown in Figure 3.5 [Wald $\chi^2(13)$ = 29.6, p = .005]. Respondents at Polk chose Health Care System Problems as a top-two problem less frequently than average [10 percent compared with 22 percent; Wald $\chi^2(1)$ = 15.45, $p < .001$], and respondents at Meade chose Health Care System Problems as a top-two problem more frequently than average [34 percent; Wald $\chi^2(1)$ = 6.52, p = .01]. Garrisons did not significantly differ in the number of Health Care System issues selected.

Summary of Garrison Context and Health Care System Problems

The subject of health care elicited much discussion among focus group members. The military health system was seen as a seriously overburdened system and a leading

Figure 3.5
Garrison Differences in Percentage of Respondents Who Chose Health Care System Problems as a Top-Two Problem

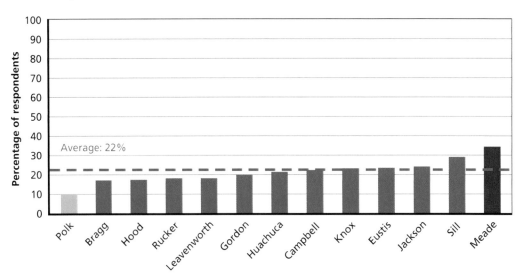

NOTE: All survey respondents were soldiers (N = 7,092). The percentage of respondents who chose Health Care System Problems as a top-two problem was significantly lower at Fort Polk and significantly higher at Fort Meade compared to the overall Army average (22 percent). All comparisons controlled for paygrade and family status.
RAND RR2148A-3.5

source of problems, with inordinately long wait times to see a medical professional and many bureaucratic barriers to care. Problems with the health care system have a ripple effect, causing soldiers to miss duty time and forcing others to cover for them in their absence. As shown in the survey results and discussed in our focus group findings, Meade respondents identified some specific health care system challenges. Views on the quality of care tended to be mixed. Other commonly cited problems were those who manipulated the health care system to avoid undesirable duties and those who were attempting to build a case for medical retirement.

Relationship Problems and Spouse's Well-Being
Focus Group Findings
Focus group participants reported relationship problems as a significant issue for soldiers and their families. The top contributors to relationship problems discussed in focus groups were deployment periods, shift-work schedules, and the lack of understanding of military language and culture among Army spouses. Senior officers and NCO focus group participants mentioned that relationship problems were particularly an issue for younger soldiers.

Not surprisingly, **focus group participants named deployment periods as a major challenge for relationships and marriages.** FRG representatives at both Fort

Meade and Fort Gordon described how it is difficult to track and engage family members in resources and support groups because many units at these installations deployed soldiers individually or in pairs (e.g., to embed with and support other units); families of deployed soldiers lack the kinship that can develop among families when an entire unit deploys together. FRG leaders described "a rotating door of people being deployed at all times in small numbers, so we don't see the same process with predeployment that we had before." Another FRG representative at Fort Meade mentioned the need for a predeployment process through the garrison that directly connects the spouses of deployed soldiers to the FRG and other support networks. Participants agreed on how crucial these support groups could be for spouse and family well-being, especially when it is the first deployment.

Respondents from the Fort Hood focus groups identified divorce and separation as some of the negative results of long-term deployments and suggested the need for more marriage counselors on post.

In terms of supportive resources for relationships, respondents tended to focus on chaplains and chaplain-led outreach programs and retreats, such as the Strong Bonds program,[10] which was singled out as a helpful resource for supporting relationships. For many, chaplains also appeared to be the go-to resource for relationship problems. An FRG representative at Fort Meade summarized the issue as follows: "When you don't have chaplains in your unit, you don't get those types of things [Strong Bonds retreats], and—well, relationships are tough. And relationships in the Army are even tougher." Respondents agreed that when soldiers are not connected to these programs or other counseling resources for help with relationship issues, many turn to divorce or separation.

Participants drew linkages between nonstandard and sometimes variable schedules (e.g., periods of intensive training or shift work) and strains on their relationships and spouses. Both soldier and Army spouse focus group participants expressed that shift-work schedules and long workdays are a challenge to a healthy home life.

Relationship problems were raised as a top concern when senior officers were asked what the most common problems were for their junior soldiers and their families. Respondents described scenarios in which soldiers married after dating only a few months and then divorced a few months later. **Senior officers noted that today's young soldiers seemed particularly lacking in relationship and communication skills.** One respondent attributed this to young soldiers' not having grown up with models of healthy relationships or stable families. Focus group participants pointed out that many of these soldiers have parents that have married multiple times, and these soldiers will go into marriage "without really knowing what marriage means for them."

---

[10] Strong Bonds is a chaplain-led program that aims to increase individual soldier and family member readiness through relationship education and skills training (Army Strong Bonds Program, 2017).

Another factor that respondents felt contributed to both relationship problems and spouse well-being issues was the lack of communication between soldiers and their spouses regarding military life and culture. For example, spouses may be unaware of the conventions of living on post, such as stopping to face the flag during retreat. This lack of awareness often extends to information that could be helpful to spouses as they acclimate, such as information about Army resources. Focus group respondents agreed that adjusting to military language and culture can be a challenge and that soldiers have some trouble explaining the work they do to their spouses. Respondents explained that there is a language challenge—"maybe the soldier doesn't know how to translate 'Army speak' into what the spouse can understand"—and suggested that there is a need to improve communication with family members about Army life.

Respondents saw part of understanding Army language and culture as having an awareness of or knowing where to find out about Army resources. Senior soldiers noted a frequent issue of young soldiers deploying and leaving spouses behind who are disconnected from Army resources because of the spouses' lack of knowledge of and acculturation to Army life. Focus groups with Army spouses discussed how living at installations away from their family and close friends can be difficult and often lead to them feeling lonely and depressed. Lack of camaraderie among families on installations was noted at several of the sites we visited; respondents sometimes contrasted installation life at their current duty station with the stronger sense of community they had experienced at Fort Bragg or Fort Lewis, for example.

Army spouse participants across the focus groups shared their experiences and **struggles with searching for network groups on post and wanting to connect with other Army spouses.** Some focus group participants had never heard of an FRG, and others mentioned previous bad experiences or attending an FRG event with the hope of making new friends but feeling out of place as new Army spouses. Respondents expressed the need for more inclusive groups for new spouses on post, particularly during deployment periods. Some resource providers and FRG leaders noted that restrictions on obtaining spouses' contact information limited their ability to reach out to spouses directly. They speculated that being able to do this, via email, for example, would potentially sidestep the issue of needing the soldier to be the primary conduit of information to spouses and partners.

Among the garrisons we visited, there was not a perceptible difference in the extent to which relationship and spouse well-being problems were considered a leading or most common problem. In general, junior enlisted soldiers were less likely than NCOs to raise relationship problems as a challenge faced by soldiers and their families. Not surprisingly, spouse well-being and relationship problems were a larger focus of the spouse interviews and focus groups than the soldier focus groups.

Survey Results

Garrison differences in Relationship Problems as a top-two problem are shown in Figure 3.6 [Wald $\chi^2(13)$ = 24.2, p = .03]. Controlling for paygrade and family status,

Figure 3.6
Garrison Differences in Percentage of Respondents Who Chose Relationship Problems as a Top-Two Problem

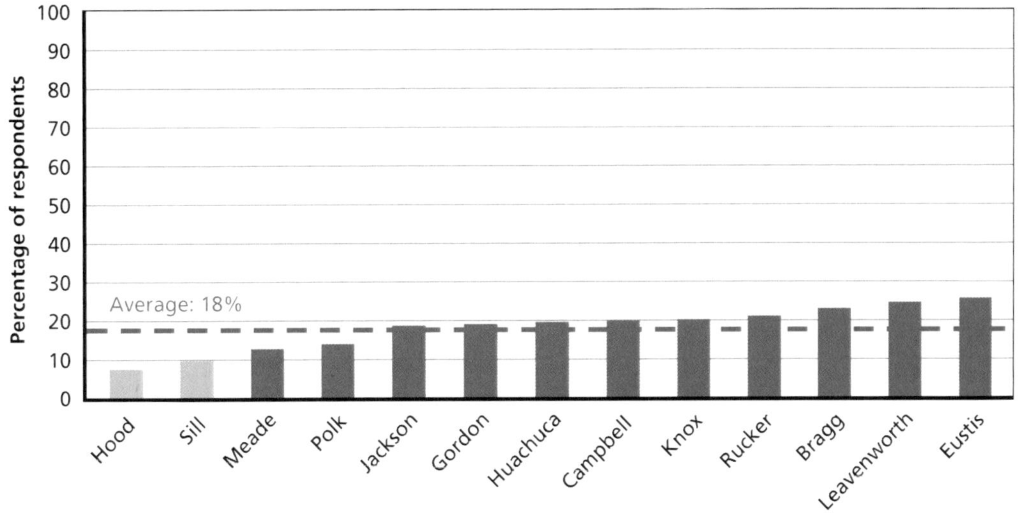

NOTE: All survey respondents were soldiers (N = 7,092). The percentage of respondents who chose Relationship Problems as a top-two problem was significantly lower at Fort Hood and Fort Sill compared to the overall Army average (18 percent). All comparisons controlled for paygrade and family status.
RAND RR2148A-3.6

respondents at Hood and Sill chose Relationship Problems as a top-two problem less frequently than average [8 percent and 10 percent compared with 18 percent; Wald $\chi^2(1)$ = 5.97 and 9.18, ps = .01 and .002, respectively]. Garrisons did not significantly differ in the number of relationship issues selected.

Spouse's Well-Being Survey Results
Garrisons did not significantly differ in the number of spouse well-being issues selected or the choice of Spouse's Well-Being as a top-two problem.

Summary of Garrison Context and Problems with Relationships and Spouse Well-Being
Deployments were seen as a major challenge to spouses. Often, the spouse had no contacts within the military that he or she could turn to for advice or assistance. Simultaneously, unit or post organizations that could provide help had difficulty tracking or engaging with family members of deployed soldiers. Thus, even when help was available, it was hard to bring to bear. Unusual and variable work schedules also strained relationships. These included intensive training, which kept units in the field for long periods, and shift work, which kept some spouses from interacting other than sporadically. More senior respondents noted a lack of communication among young couples, both about resolving problems and about the ins and outs of military culture, which can seem quite foreign to young spouses. Although survey respondents from Fort Hood

were less likely to prioritize relationship problems, the respondents in Fort Hood focus groups reflected more general concerns rather than any themes specific to the location.

Child Well-Being
Focus Group Findings

A leading problem for soldiers with children, and the main focus within the category of Child Well-Being, was day care for young children. The major concern with on-post Child Development Centers (CDCs) reported by respondents was waiting lists; many soldiers and spouses shared stories of being on waiting lists for many months and even years. Several female soldiers without children mentioned that the only thing they had been told about Army childcare was to get on the waiting list immediately after they find out they are pregnant. Dual-military and single-parent respondents reported that long day care waiting lists were particularly frustrating and forced them to seek outside resources such as off-post day care or Army spouses who ran certified home day care programs.[11]

For parents with children enrolled in Army CDCs, the hours of operation emerged as an issue affecting at least some soldiers at each location. For example, respondents noted that shift work (particularly in intelligence and medical units) and the common occurrence of early PT times for some units (especially Advanced Individual Training instructors and in warmer climates, where PT might begin very early to avoid morning heat) made it difficult to drop off and pick up their children from childcare because CDCs do not offer care 24 hours a day.[12] One soldier expressed the frustration by saying, "We are supposed to be soldiers 24 hours a day but the lack of support resources makes that impossible." Focus group respondents across installations agreed on the conflict this creates between work and parental responsibilities, especially for single parents and dual-military families, who must have contingencies in place for when one spouse is on temporary duty or deployed. NCOs described soldiers who need to bring their children to work or who have sleeping children in the car while doing PT, and they universally agreed that this was not a good situation for anyone. Respondents also described variability in the chain of command's understanding and flexibility when they are facing parental responsibilities. For example, one NCO argued that leadership should know the day care operating hours and plan accordingly so that soldiers in their unit are able to focus on training, rather than on cobbling together childcare solutions or bringing their children to formation. The NCO stressed the need for leadership to be more supportive when such resources are not available.

---

[11] OACSIM notes that the Army has a robust program that offers fee assistance to families when there are long waiting lists or for families who are geographically dispersed. Approximately 9,500 families are enrolled in this program.

[12] OACSIM notes that most of the Army's childcare centers are open more than the required 12 hours (about 80 percent), and all CDCs will extend their operating hours to meet mission requirements on an as-needed basis.

NCOs admitted that they had a great deal of flexibility when dealing with soldiers who had childcare challenges and that, although they were often sympathetic, for some soldiers it could become grounds for being disciplined or eliminated from the service. Soldiers at Fort Gordon and Fort Huachuca described how Family Care Plans, which are intended for deployment and long-term absence, could be challenged as deficient if a soldier has childcare issues, but they stated that the way the plans are designed, they really are not effective for planning around shift-work schedules or limited day care hours of operation. Overall, participants agreed that child day care is a crucial resource for parents in the military and directly affects soldier and mission readiness.

Survey Results

Garrisons did not significantly differ in the number of Child Well-Being issues selected or the choice of Child Well-Being as a top-two problem.

Summary of Garrison Context and Problems with Child Well-Being

With regard to childcare problems, the extent to which garrisons relied on shift work or required early PT times (because of Advanced Individual Training schedules or warm climate) affected the types of childcare problems experienced by soldiers and their families. The large majority of childcare issues raised were related to childcare for children younger than school age. A number of institutional issues—hours for CDCs, for example—exacerbated issues associated with childcare, particularly for joint military couples or single parents.

Summary of Findings Regarding Problems

With regard to the survey analysis by garrison, prioritized problem areas chosen by soldiers at a local level tended to reflect the earlier aggregate Army-level analysis: Military Practices and Culture, Soldier's Well-Being, and Work-Life Balance were chosen the most frequently. The focus groups generated a rich discussion of the types of problems soldiers and their families face, which covered somewhat different ground from the survey results. This difference in part reflected the different focus of the discussions, which were more an exploration of the process of coping with different problems than an attempt to prioritize only problems that were the most challenging in the prior year. Thus, focus groups spoke to military practices and culture, work-life balance, and soldier well-being, but health care and childcare system problems were also frequently mentioned. Quite often, neither the survey findings nor the focus groups spoke to a particular type of problem being localized. Rather, our findings illustrated that certain problems are typical, regardless of location.

Despite the similarities in prioritized problem domains across garrisons, there was significant variance in the selection of some specific problem domains on the survey. For example, compared to the average, Health Care System Problems was more frequently chosen as a top problem by respondents at Fort Meade, was ranked as one of the top three problems by Fort Meade respondents, and was frequently mentioned by focus group respondents at Fort Meade. In addition, although Military Practices and Culture and Work-Life Balance were ranked as top problems across garrisons, they were chosen more frequently by respondents at Fort Bragg and Fort Hood, respectively, compared with the average. The age, quality, and quantity of on-post housing and barracks vary by installation; therefore, the garrison context has a strong relationship to the types of housing problems that soldiers and their families will experience. This was evident in the survey analyses, in which Huachuca respondents listed fewer Household Management issues overall, while Polk respondents were more likely to choose Household Management as a top problem and Bragg respondents were less likely to choose it as a top problem. Focus group results added additional depth to our examination of the nature and extent of housing issues experienced by soldiers and their families. Thus, although the theme that was clearest regarding problems faced by soldiers and families was one of a shared Army experience, local differences do shine through as well.

Needs for Addressing Problems

For each of the top-two problems selected by respondents on the survey, respondents were prompted to select what types of help or support they needed most to deal with these problems. Respondents could select as many needs as applied to their problem. If they chose more than two needs for either problem, they were asked to prioritize the top two needs they had for addressing the problem.

We did not explore needs for addressing problems in focus groups because we felt the discussion flowed naturally from the problems soldiers and their families experienced to the process of problem solving and resources used. However, no focus group participants discussed particular types of help for solving problems that were simply unavailable; rather, discussions in focus groups seemed to reflect availability of the right types of help but also various barriers to their use (reported in the resource use section later).

Table 3.3 displays the three most cited problem-need pairs chosen by respondents at each garrison. Although the top problem-need pairs reported by soldiers at some garrisons were relatively evenly distributed (e.g., at Forts Bragg and Eustis), the top problem-need pair at other garrisons was cited by a greater percentage of soldiers relative to other problem-need pairs. For example, at Fort Hood, 31 percent of soldiers reported that they needed advice for problems with Military Practices and Culture. At Fort Huachuca, 28 percent of soldiers reported that they needed activities to deal with problems with their own well-being. At Fort Meade, two problem-need pairs were more prominent: 31 percent of soldiers reported that they needed emotional support to deal with problems with their own well-being, and 26 percent reported that they needed an advocate for problems with military practices and culture. These data sug-

Table 3.3
Most Cited Problem-Need Pairs and Percentage Cited by Garrison Respondents

	Problem-Need Pair 1	Problem-Need Pair 2	Problem-Need Pair 3
Bragg	Relationships—emotional support, 21%	Military Practices and Culture—specific info, 20%	Military Practices and Culture—counseling, 19%
Campbell	Military Practices and Culture—specific info, 25%	Military Practices and Culture—general info, 22%	Military Practices and Culture—other need, 18%
Eustis	Relationships—emotional support, 17%	Relationships—activities, 16%	Military Practices and Culture—general info, 16%
Gordon	Military Practices and Culture—general info, 19%	Own Well-Being—counseling, 12%	Health Care—other need, 11%
Hood	Military Practices and Culture—advice, 31%	Work-Life Balance—advice, 20%	Military Practices and Culture—counseling, 15%
Huachuca	Own Well-Being—activities, 28%	Spouse Well-Being—emotional support, 15%	Spouse Well-Being—counseling, 13%
Jackson	Work-Life Balance—other need, 13%	Military Practices and Culture—general info, 12%	Relationships—activities, 11%
Knox	Household Management—other need, 20%	Financial or Legal—advocate, 19%	Household Management—advocate, 17%
Leavenworth	Military Practices and Culture—general info, 13%	Own Well-Being—activities, 11%	Work-Life Balance—other need, 10%
Meade	Own Well-Being—emotional support, 31%	Military Practices and Culture—advocate, 26%	Own Well-Being—advice, 18%
Polk	Own Well-Being—activities, 18%	Military Practices and Culture—specific info, 16%	Military Practices and Culture—general info, 14%
Rucker	Military Practices and Culture—general info, 16%	Military Practices and Culture—advice, 14%	Own Well-Being—emotional support, 12%
Sill	Health Care—other need, 17%	Military Practices and Culture—general info, 13%	Military Practices and Culture—specific info, 13%

NOTE: All survey respondents were soldiers (N = 7,092). Percentages are within garrison for respondents who reported problems and associated needs. Since respondents could list up to two needs for each of their two prioritized problems, for a total of four problem-need pairs, percentages may add up to more than 100 percent.

Table 3.4
The Three Needs Most Cited by Respondents at Each Garrison

	Advice	Activities	General Info	Counseling	Advocate	Emotional Support	Specific Info
Bragg			26%			27%	29%
Campbell		19%	22%				20%
Eustis		24%	26%			22%	
Gordon		22%	25%	24%			
Hood	37%	23%		22%			
Huachuca	18%	33%	24%				
Jackson	22%	24%	24%				
Knox	22%			20%	25%		
Leavenworth		21%	25%	21%			
Meade	42%				38%	37%	
Polk	18%	25%		18%			
Rucker	22%	24%	23%				
Sill	21%		21%			22%	

NOTE: All survey respondents were soldiers (N = 7,092). Percentages are for respondents within garrisons. Respondents could choose up to two top problem areas, so percentages may total more than 100 percent.

gest a need for a particular type of resource to address a particular type of concern at given locations, though survey responses should be considered in the context of installation offerings, priorities, and budget. Where a variety of needs are associated with a given problem domain at a particular installation, respondents see a variety of solutions that might address their issues.

Examining needs across problem domains, the most frequently cited needs for addressing problems varied considerably across garrisons (see Table 3.4). The needs for advice, activities, and general information were all fairly common across garrisons, but other needs varied. Specifically, counseling was a top need at Forts Gordon, Hood, Knox, Leavenworth, and Polk; emotional support was a top need at Forts Bragg, Eustis, Meade, and Sill; an advocate was a top need at Forts Knox and Meade; and specific information was a top need at Forts Bragg and Campbell. The general pattern of findings suggests that there is a need for information and interpersonal help such as advice, counseling, and emotional support that is relatively consistent regardless of installation.

Figure 3.7
Garrison Differences in Percentage of Respondents Who Chose Specific Information as a Prioritized Need to Address Their Problems

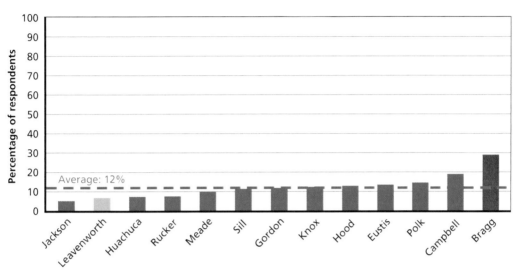

NOTE: All survey respondents were soldiers (N = 7,092). The percentage of respondents who chose specific information as a prioritized need was significantly lower at Fort Leavenworth and significantly higher at Fort Bragg compared to the overall Army average (12 percent). All comparisons controlled for paygrade and family status.
RAND RR2148A-3.7

To look for differences by garrison, we next used multiple logistic regressions to analyze the percentage of respondents who cited each need. The analysis controlled for paygrade and family status, and results revealed some significant comparisons where garrisons differed from the overall average.

As shown in Figure 3.7, garrisons differed in how likely respondents were to need specific information to address their top problems [Wald $\chi^2(13)$ = 27.21, p = .01]. Respondents at Bragg were more likely than average to need specific information [29 percent compared with 12 percent; Wald $\chi^2(1)$ = 9.17, p = .003], and respondents at Leavenworth were less likely than average to need specific information to address their problem [7 percent; Wald $\chi^2(1)$ = 7.02, p = .008]. Respondents at Jackson had a lower percentage than those at Leavenworth (5 percent), but only 16 respondents at Jackson chose specific information as one of their top needs, which creates additional error for the statistical tests. Thus, although there was too much variability among respondents at Jackson for the statistical test to cross the threshold of significance, soldiers at Jackson were the least likely among the garrisons to indicate that they needed specific information to help address their problems.

As shown in Figure 3.8, garrisons differed in how likely respondents were to need an advocate to address their top problems [Wald $\chi^2(13)$ = 26.4, p = .01]. Respondents

Figure 3.8
**Garrison Differences in Percentage of Respondents Who Chose an Advocate as a
Prioritized Need to Address Their Problems**

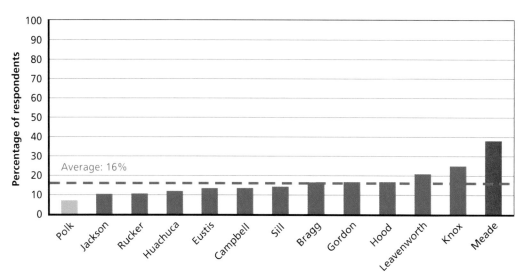

NOTE: All survey respondents were soldiers (N = 7,092). The percentage of respondents who chose an
advocate as a prioritized need was significantly lower at Fort Polk and significantly higher at Fort
Meade compared to the overall Army average (16 percent). All comparisons controlled for paygrade
and family status.
RAND RR2148A-3.8

at Meade were more likely than average to need an advocate [38 percent compared
with 16 percent; Wald $\chi^2(1)$ = 7.64, p = .006], and respondents at Polk were less likely
than average to need an advocate to address their problem [7 percent; Wald $\chi^2(1)$ =
6.59, p = .01].

No significant omnibus garrison effects emerged for any of the other needs (all
ps > .06).

Resource Use

As described by Sims, Trail, et al. (2017), respondents who reported problems and needs
on the survey also reported whether they accessed different military and nonmilitary
resources to deal with their needs. Although the vast majority of respondents reported
using resources to help cope with their needs (85 percent), some respondents had problems and needs but reported using no resources to help address those needs. The proportion of respondents who used resources did not significantly differ by garrison.

Of those who used resources to meet their needs, the number and type of
resources used varied by garrison. Tables 3.5 and 3.6 display the military and nonmilitary resources included in the survey, along with the percentage of respondents who

Table 3.5
Percentage of Respondents Accessing Military Resources to Address Needs, by Garrison

Military Resource	Army Average	Bragg	Campbell	Eustis	Gordon	Hood	Huachuca	Jackson	Knox	Leavenworth	Meade	Polk	Rucker	Sill
FRG	13	13	16	11	8	17	9	10	12	6	10	20	12	13
Unit members not in the chain of command	49	60	53	42	50	43	45	42	50	36	72	61	46	54
Installation MWR (e.g., recreation or sports services such as intramural sports, libraries, or post gymnasium)	24	35	15	28	24	25	42	15	24	24	17	39	32	22
ACS (e.g., financial services, relocation assistance, and family services)	22	27	9	23	21	17	43	20	23	18	27	32	20	20
Child and Youth Services (for example, on-post childcare or youth sports)	12	14	2	11	12	7	13	10	11	17	6	13	13	10
Army OneSource, post homepage, or other military Internet resources or social media (such as Twitter or Facebook)	18	21	14	21	22	21	21	18	13	19	21	17	18	15
Chain of command (squad leaders, NCOs/officers, rear detachment commanders, Sexual Harassment/Assault Response and Prevention advocates, or designated points of contact for family issues)	50	61	59	32	54	73	62	49	52	37	73	34	47	53
Chaplain or members of military religious or spiritual group	21	16	26	19	32	21	26	21	26	15	15	28	19	18
Counselor or doctor provided by the military	36	33	29	37	38	34	35	30	35	38	32	29	30	52
Relief or aid society (AER)[a]	5	6	7	6	3	3	4	15	2	1	6	8	4	6
Other military contacts	13	5	5	12	14	10	13	18	10	20	9	7	16	9

NOTE: All survey respondents were soldiers (N = 7,092). Percentages highlighted in green are significantly below the overall average resource use, and percentages highlighted in red are significantly higher than the overall average resource use. All comparisons controlled for paygrade and family status.
[a] Cell sizes were too small to calculate reliable estimates of difference from the overall mean.

Table 3.6
Percentage of Respondents Accessing Nonmilitary Resources to Address Needs, by Garrison

Nonmilitary Resources	Army Average	Bragg	Campbell	Eustis	Gordon	Hood	Huachuca	Jackson	Knox	Leavenworth	Meade	Polk	Rucker	Sill
Government or community resources for family services (e.g., Temporary Assistance for Needy Families, Special Supplemental Nutrition Program for Women, Infants, and Children, public library, Head Start, or community center)[a]	7	7	4	8	9	3	3	1	11	10	9	10	5	9
Private clubs, organizations, or recreation or fitness centers	17	16	15	25	12	5	27	8	12	14	16	14	24	15
Private, off-post childcare[a]	7	11	6	8	6	5	8	5	8	10	6	4	11	7
Religious or spiritual group or leader	17	17	17	21	16	15	8	21	19	16	13	27	24	18
Private doctor or counselor	16	16	6	15	15	14	18	15	13	18	15	8	14	26
Internet resources (such as WebMD, Google, Craigslist, Wikipedia, Yahoo!, Twitter, or Facebook)	30	43	21	24	32	28	30	23	16	28	34	42	33	34
Personal networks (friends or family)	46	60	36	48	47	47	48	35	25	38	68	57	52	49
Other nonmilitary contacts[a]	5	3	1	4	1	3	2	8	7	8	7	3	4	3

NOTE: All survey respondents were soldiers (N = 7,092). Percentages highlighted in green are significantly below the overall average resource use, and percentages highlighted in red are significantly higher than the overall average resource use. All comparisons controlled for paygrade and family status.

[a] Cell sizes were too small to calculate reliable estimates of difference from the overall mean.

indicated that they accessed each resource to address their needs (respondents could choose more than one resource for each problem-need pair). As shown in Table 3.5, respondents at Fort Meade (red-shaded cell) were significantly more likely than average to access both unit members not in their chain of command and those in their chain of command to help deal with their needs. In contrast, respondents at Forts Eustis and Polk were less likely than average (green-shaded cells) to resort to their chain of command to help address their needs. Respondents at Fort Campbell were less likely than average to access ACS to address their needs. As shown in Table 3.6, respondents at Fort Meade were also more likely than average to access their personal networks to address their needs. Respondents at Leavenworth were significantly less likely than average to access their personal networks to address their needs. Finally, respondents at Fort Hood were less likely than average to access "private clubs, organizations, or recreation or fitness centers" to address their needs.

We next examined the number of military and nonmilitary resources used by respondents to address their needs. Among those who used resources, garrisons differed on the overall number of resources used [$F(13, 4801) = 1.74, p = .048$]. Respondents at Fort Leavenworth used significantly fewer resources than average [6.3 compared with 7.6; $t(4801) = -3.09, p = .002$]. Similarly, garrisons differed on the number of *military* resources used to address their needs [$F(13, 4801) = 1.76, p = .044$]. Respondents at Fort Leavenworth used fewer military resources to help address their needs than average [3.9 compared with 4.9; $t(4801) = -3.65, p < .001$]. Garrisons did not significantly differ from average on the number of nonmilitary resources used to address needs. Thus, with the exception of Fort Leavenworth, resource use was relatively uniform across garrisons.

For the resources that respondents used to help with their needs, we asked how satisfied they were with the help they received (Sims, Trail, et al., 2017). Garrisons did not significantly differ from average on overall satisfaction with resources or satisfaction with military or nonmilitary resources. This finding suggests that, regardless of the differences in problem type or needs among soldiers at different garrisons, satisfaction with the help received from resources did not vary across garrisons.

Because of the smaller sample size for respondents who used specific resources, we could not reliably calculate garrison differences in satisfaction for each resource.

Another way to evaluate satisfaction with resources is to examine whether the resources used by soldiers actually met their needs or left some unmet (Sims, Trail, et al., 2017). In our problem-solving and coping context, unmet needs do not mean an absence of problems and needs, which are unavoidable. Rather, we wanted to determine whether soldiers and families were unable to find satisfactory help for their problems and needs. Resources that were rated by respondents as meeting their needs "well" or "very well" were coded as having met the soldier's needs. Otherwise, the resource was coded as *not* having met the respondent's needs. We looked across resources used for a given problem-need pair, and if at least one of them did meet the needs (that is,

Figure 3.9
Garrison Differences in Percentage of Respondents with Unmet Needs

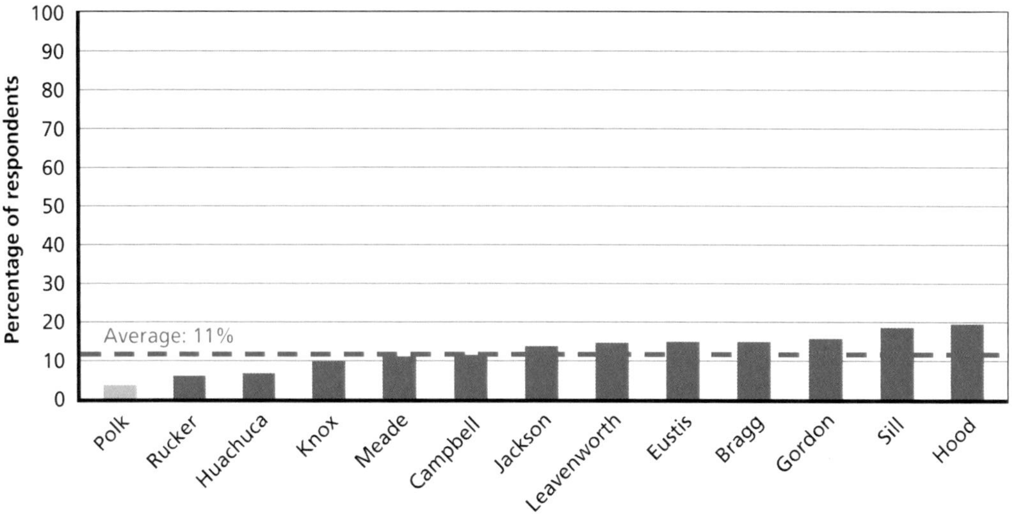

NOTE: All survey respondents were soldiers (N = 7,092). The percentage of respondents with unmet needs was significantly lower at Fort Polk compared to the overall Army average (11 percent). All comparisons controlled for paygrade and family status.
RAND RR2148A-3.9

was rated as meeting needs "well" or "very well"), we considered the overall need likely to have been met. Only those who rated all resources as performing less than "well" at meeting needs were considered to have their needs unmet. By this measure, 11 percent of respondents overall had unmet needs. As shown in Figure 3.9, there was a significant garrison effect [Wald $\chi^2(13) = 26.73$, $p = .015$], where respondents at Fort Polk were less likely than average to have unmet needs [Wald $\chi^2(1) = 11.38$, $p < .001$]. No other garrisons significantly differed from average.

Common Gateways to Resources: Findings from Focus Groups

The discussion guide for the focus groups included questions that focused on how respondents found out about and got information about resources, impressions of which resources were used most often, experiences of using resources, and barriers to and facilitators of resource use. In this section we describe three resources (ACS, chain of command, and mental and behavioral health services, including chaplains) that were well known and commonly used by our respondents. Furthermore, these resources were frequently described as a first point of contact when seeking out help for a problem, and they were likely to refer soldiers to other resources when they themselves could not provide the help needed.

ACS

ACS was mentioned frequently as a particularly popular and useful resource for soldiers and their families. In general, soldiers spoke positively of ACS as a resource and were able to name specific services within ACS they had used or directed soldiers to (e.g., AER, Exceptional Family Member Program, or financial counseling). Because ACS has so many functions and programs, some respondents described needing to do what one respondent called "detective work" to connect with the right resource within ACS. However, respondents generally agreed that ACS service providers were knowledgeable about other ACS programs and could help connect them with the right person, even if the first contact made by the soldier was the wrong office or program for the issue.

Chain of Command

Chain of command was frequently mentioned not only as a resource for information about resources but also as a resource in and of itself. Soldiers pointed to their commanders as teachers and mentors, as reliable sources of information, and as gateways to different resources. Respondents—both junior soldiers and those in the chain of command themselves—recognized how much effect a senior soldier can have on young soldiers' experiences and outcomes in the Army. However, senior soldiers acknowledge that the time spent mentoring younger soldiers has declined in recent years, as a result both of what they view as excessive competing demands on their time and of cultural shifts that deter younger soldiers from seeking help from them.

Despite chain of command being a prominent resource for soldiers and their families, not all comments about the chain of command were positive. Some younger soldiers reported being hesitant to reach out to their leadership because of concerns that they would face stigma, concerns that their leaders would not be supportive, or concerns for their own privacy when dealing with leaders who were perceived as indiscreet. From the other perspective, some senior soldiers mentioned being hesitant to *offer* help, explaining that they were already stretched thin across too many soldiers, and that asking questions about or digging deeper into problems might raise issues that they did not have time or resources to help with. Both NCOs and officers raised concerns about sensitivity in today's Army and expressed worry that calling out a problem that they notice in a soldier (to encourage or to help the solder deal with it) might be perceived as harassment or an invasion of privacy.

However, respondents noted variation in how willing junior soldiers were to receive help with problems. Some senior soldiers mentioned not wanting to be *too* helpful a resource because they felt that soldiers needed to learn to be independent and to at least attempt to manage their problems on their own. There was some suggestion that providing help too quickly—for example, with navigating Army procedures—might propagate a pattern of dependence that respondents described seeing in some junior soldiers.

Mental and Behavioral Health Resources, Including Chaplains

Soldiers spoke fairly consistently about the value of the mental health services and embedded behavioral health in particular. There were more inconsistent views on the awareness, quality, and values of Military and Family Life Counselors, with some respondents describing them as very valuable and others unaware that they even existed. Access was named as the leading barrier to mental health services. Soldiers mentioned a shortage of providers, long wait times to get an appointment, and lack of childcare as barriers to using mental health resources, including military and family life counselors. Some concerns were tied to the different degrees of privacy afforded to soldiers by the different mental health service providers and the extent to which recorded health information could become a liability for them. For example, respondents felt that seeking mental health resources might put their security clearances at risk, and that this fear could be a deterrent to seeking out the mental health services they may need. Despite efforts in place to reduce the stigma surrounding mental health issues, it was still sometimes raised as a concern. Although leaders were generally supportive of soldiers seeking out mental health services, there was also discussion of inappropriate use of mental health services, such as soldiers malingering or "shopping" for behavioral health diagnoses (e.g., post-traumatic stress disorder) as a way to be medically retired from the Army. Given leaders' perception that abuse of mental health services is common, it is understandable that soldiers may feel the need to be cautious in their use of mental health resources.

Chaplains also played a prominent role in providing support to soldiers and families who were dealing with problems. Notably, from soldiers' reports, day-to-day chaplain support of a unit goes far beyond spiritual support. Rather, the chaplains assist soldiers and families across a range of issues and serve as gateways to other, more specialized Army resources. Both soldiers and resource providers discussed how the guarantee of anonymity when talking to a chaplain was attractive to soldiers who were looking for someone to talk to. One service provider and several soldier respondents discussed a general impression that going to a chaplain for counseling or advice was less stigmatized than accessing other resources, particularly mental health resources. The model of an embedded chaplain was described as sometimes beneficial, because soldiers would become familiar with someone over time and therefore be more likely to come into contact with him or her and engage in formal or informal counseling. However, one respondent mentioned that chaplains who are affiliated with units are sometimes avoided—a soldier might go to a chaplain outside his or her unit—when dealing with unit-specific problems.

In focus groups with service providers, we heard about some innovations and new approaches that they were implementing in the context of mental health. Some spoke of the importance of changing the narrative to *prevention* as opposed to *punishment* in situations involving mental health and behaviors stemming from mental health issues. Others described the more holistic approach they were taking to mental health services and their openness to integrating new tools such as yoga instead of relying strictly on conventional treatment (e.g., medications). In addition, the service providers we spoke with seemed committed to connecting with and sharing information across multiple stakeholders—both on the installations and off—in the interest of soldiers' mental health and well-being. For example, some service providers talked about the importance of integrating spouses into conversations about soldiers' mental health, with some suggesting that spouses should be viewed as the front line when it comes to identifying mental health issues and providing care.

Multiple Resource Use

Survey results showed that soldiers approached an average of 2.8 different resources to deal with each of their needs. We used the focus groups to get a better understanding of the dynamic and reasoning behind multiple resource use. When respondents were asked why soldiers might approach multiple resources in an attempt to meet the needs of themselves and their families, they offered several different explanations, such as having complex problems that required attention from different providers, approaching multiple offices because they do not know where to go, and being misdirected and rerouted among the different service providers.

Focus group participants observed that some soldiers have complex, multidimensional problems that require attention from different services. This situation could result from multiple problems that are interconnected or from a single problem that "gets out of hand" when it is not handled in a timely fashion. For instance, chain of command may send a soldier for behavioral health counseling upon noticing certain behaviors, but once in counseling, the soldier may realize that there is more to the problem. As described by one respondent, "It may just be that in peeling back the onion these soldiers realize they need more and more care from different providers." In other cases the soldiers may just wait too long to get help and end up with compounded problems (e.g., financial problems that generate other problems, such as letters of indebtedness and loss of credit, if neglected).

Respondents also mentioned that soldiers do not always know where to go for help with their problems, so they may end up going to a few different resources before they find the right match. Although this is most common for the junior soldiers, participants agreed that soldiers look for services once they become relevant to their needs, so finding the correct resource may require some trial and error. Given the timing of resource seeking—namely, when a soldier or family member is experiencing a problem—this trial-and-error process may be occurring at the least opportune time. Respondents concurred that some of this bouncing around could be avoided if there were more coordination and communication among service providers, and unfortunately respondents described experiences in which resource providers were unable to direct them appropriately (e.g., "The resource providers, if it is not about their program, they don't really know to tell you where to go"). Thus, individuals are either misdirected or left to figure out for themselves where to go. This fragmentation and lack of communication between service providers can prolong the soldiers' process in receiving necessary services or completely discourage them from trying to use on-post resources.

Participants in the Fort Hood service provider group mentioned a few efforts to work with other resources on post but believed that there was a greater need to do more of this across the installation. Resource providers tend to assume that their information sharing or presentations are useful, important, and a productive use of soldiers' time. (Given that their typical interaction with soldiers is with those who use resources, it is one way to reach the larger potential population who might ultimately need what they provide.) Soldier respondents suggested that service providers should be required to attend some overview of all other services on post similar to the in-process brief that soldiers attend when they first come on post. They shared that many service providers attend the brief but will only stay to present the services they provide and dismiss themselves without hearing about the other resources on post. Soldier respondents agreed that a more standard knowledge base and the proactive collaboration across service providers and offices would create a more robust and less intimidating network of resources. A better coordination system among the resources on post could reduce the time the soldiers spend trying to find the right resources for their needs. Furthermore, it would create a more comprehensive way of delivering the line of support the soldiers need to meet their mission readiness.

Information About Resources

Survey Findings
The survey asked respondents who listed problems, "What is the best way to get information to you about services available to help meet your needs?" (see Sims, Trail, et al., 2017, for more information). The most frequently reported preferred method of getting information about resources was through an email from the unit leader: 43 percent of respondents selected this method. The next most frequently reported preferred method was through friends, family, or coworkers (24 percent). About 22 percent of respondents reported preferring to receive information through social media (e.g., Twitter, Facebook, or a phone app).

Focus Group Findings
Focus group respondents were asked to describe how they heard about Army resources and where they went for information about resources when they had a problem. Focus group participants were both resource *consumers* (i.e., soldiers and their families) and resource *providers* (different organizations on the installation), so in addition to provid-

ing information on how soldiers and their families find out about resources, our findings speak to how resources and service providers currently disseminate information and updates (e.g., what they believe is most effective in reaching potential program users). Participants across several focus groups endorsed the idea that effective methods exist for getting information in front of people but stated that ensuring soldiers pay attention to messages or internalize information was the bigger challenge.[13]

Multiple Sources of Information About Resources Exist

Across installations and participant groups, a central theme was that soldiers and their families gather information—and service providers share information—through multiple channels as opposed to just relying on a single source. One spouse respondent, for example, mentioned drawing information from the Internet, Facebook, the installation's ACS magazine, and a trade journal published by the Armed Forces Communications and Electronics Association called *Signal* magazine. Similarly, service providers and organizations at installations reported communicating their offerings through multiple channels as well. When asked what the most effective tools were for communicating with soldiers, a service provider respondent from Fort Gordon listed using Facebook, Twitter, and email, in addition to holding in-person introductions and briefings, using billboards and marquees, and sharing information through the *Fort Gordon Globe* newspaper and the Fort Gordon *FYI Magazine*. The respondent explained, "We are trying to cover all bases."

The Internet as a Source of Information About Resources

When asked how they obtained information about resources, a leading response was "the Internet," by which respondents meant using search engines or accessing the installation or resource-specific websites. Remarks from several respondents suggest that soldiers and their families, particularly younger soldiers, view Google as their starting point when they are seeking information. Google searches may lead those seeking information to the website for their installation or for particular service providers, such as the MWR website.

However, comments from respondents at the different site-visit installations seemed to indicate inconsistencies in the quality and reliability of their respective websites. There were even conflicting comments made by respondents talking about the *same* website, suggesting that implementing effective installation websites for users of all need and skill levels may be a challenge. In addition to complaints that installation websites contained broken links and were difficult to navigate, a respondent at one installation mentioned that its website was difficult to navigate on a mobile phone,

---

[13] Note also that actual resource use may actually only partially reflect the reported incidence of given challenges—we show here reported problems, associated needs, and resources sought, but from a service provider perspective, the "uptake" of provided resources naturally may only cover a small proportion of a population that could benefit.

which is an issue that likely affects how many soldiers and families experience the installation website as a resource for information.

Email and Text Messaging as Sources of Information About Resources

Regarding digital media and web-based tools for getting information about resources, there were conflicting comments about the use of email as an effective method for receiving information about resources. Although some mentioned gathering information by email, other respondents suggested that email may not have the same reach as other information-sharing mechanisms. Some respondents mentioned that younger soldiers do not check their email, while other respondents described a preference for or the perceived greater effectiveness of learning about resources through word of mouth or one-on-one instruction on where to go. A few respondents listed text messages as a reliable method of sharing and receiving information, and they referenced text alerts that were sent about emergency closings or hazards.

Social Media as a Source of Information About Resources

Respondents across all installations pointed to social media as a valuable mechanism for the dissemination and gathering of information. Among all social media platforms mentioned by respondents,[14] Facebook was by far the most frequently mentioned and emerged as a preferred forum for sharing and receiving information. However, some cautions were given about relying on social media as a tool for information sharing. While some respondents suggested that Facebook is ubiquitous, one respondent pointed out that not all soldiers routinely check Facebook or do any one thing consistently (e.g., read the post newspaper, look at the post website, or listen to Army radio). In fact, several respondents noted that tools such as Facebook are not secure at all, and although there may be "closed groups," they are still not a secure medium. Some Army units and FRG groups, out of an abundance of caution, choose not to use Facebook because of the possibility that deployment schedules and other sensitive information might be posted, so utilization as a producer, as well as a consumer, of information has complications. Additionally, one respondent pointed out that although social media, particularly Facebook, has been useful, there are still inconsistencies in how up-to-date the information is across different pages. The inconsistency on social media can be problematic; as one respondent noted, information shared via social media can be disseminated very quickly, and it therefore needs to be up to date and correct. In terms of outreach, providers did speak to the use of multiple channels, and among these they identified social media, particularly Facebook, as a good venue, echoing what we heard from soldiers and spouses with regard to that being a relatively good source of information.

---

[14] Across focus groups, respondents mentioned Facebook, Twitter, Periscope, Instagram, Pinterest, and Snap-Chat but elaborated on only Facebook and Twitter as a way that soldiers and families find out about resources.

Resources as a Source of Information About Resources

Another source of information about resources was the resources themselves. Respondents and their families described ACS a central point of contact for getting information about resources. To a lesser extent, Army OneSource and Military OneSource were resources (phone and website) that some respondents reported going to for information, although there were some complaints about the usability and accessibility of both resources. There was some discussion of the FRG as a source of information about resources. Participants' responses were conflicting, with some describing the FRG as a helpful source of information, while others felt that it was not a key pathway to getting connected to resources.

Even as soldiers and their families described resources such as ACS as a gateway, resource providers spoke of the value of "open-door" resources that could connect soldiers and families to other, more specific programs and resources. The open-door resources mentioned included NCOs. Service providers also mentioned collaborating and trying to stay abreast of what is available more broadly in order to be able to refer soldiers and families to more-specific programs as needed. These collaborations included taking opportunities for cross talk at Community Health Promotion Council meetings, for example.

Previous Knowledge as a Source of Information About Resources

Soldiers and family member respondents also described drawing on previous knowledge of Army resources when they were facing a problem, and gathering information from fellow soldiers, both peers and leadership. Existing knowledge of Army resources sometimes came from having grown up in the Army or having a spouse from an Army family, but most often respondents described a general awareness of resources as something that accrues as they become acculturated to the Army. Some respondents described this as a knowledge or awareness that creeps in over time. One respondent spouse described how her prior experience with resources formed the knowledge base of what was available: "I know where things are, but I'm coming in with experience— I know who to contact, I know how to find services."

Another respondent contrasted this gradual diffusion of information with formal education about resources and affirmed the idea that knowledge of resources and how to access them is developed through experience. He cited his own experience of never having received a briefing but explained how "coming up through the ranks, [soldiers] learn and share with [their] counterparts, battle buddies, and so on. You build an institutional knowledge over time." Not surprisingly, having consistency in the services offered across different installations helped soldiers' and families' knowledge about resources transfer between duty stations. However, some more-senior focus group respondents were aware that junior enlisted soldiers may not have had adequate time and exposure to build up the same general awareness of resources that they (more-experienced soldiers) had.

Word of Mouth as a Source of Information About Resources

In addition to the role of prior experience and exposure to the Army in helping soldiers be aware of resources, many respondents described gathering information from the people around them. Soldiers throughout the Army hierarchy report the importance of networking and asking peers what has worked for them. NCOs in particular described relying on networking, hearing personal stories, and asking friends what has worked for them, and they viewed this information gathering as a way that they could be more effective leaders to their soldiers. Word of mouth seems to be particularly important for Army spouses, who are not always included in the in-brief or orientation processes at installations. For example, one relatively new Army spouse attributed all the information she had about resources to "another mom," a neighbor in on-post housing, who had helped orient her to the installation.

Chain of Command as a Source of Information About Resources

Although there were sometimes challenges to this strategy, junior soldiers often reported turning to—or wanting to be able to turn to—their chain of command as a source of information. Some respondents spoke positively of more senior soldiers' (i.e., NCOs' or commanders') efforts to inform them of upcoming activities (e.g., a ceremony or training session) or ability to direct them to appropriate resources, but other respondents complained about poor flow of information from the top down to soldiers.

NCOs and soldiers in the chain of command within their respective units acknowledged their role in informing and supporting their soldiers' use of resources. These soldiers spoke of drawing on their prior experiences and knowledge they developed over time, as well as on input from *their* chain of command, to help the soldiers under their leadership. NCO respondents described a dynamic in which leaders are supposed to know what issues their soldiers are facing because of the relationships they develop with them. These relationships and this knowledge facilitate the appropriate sharing of information about resources that might be helpful.

Interestingly, some respondents were quick to note that social media should not be viewed as a replacement for leaders' interpersonal communications with their soldiers. Rather, on the topic of chain of command as a resource for information, there seems to be a shared interest across paygrades in the usefulness of information being disseminated during routine daily formations, in the form of announcements by the first sergeant, platoon sergeant, or service providers (e.g., chaplain).

In-Processing as a Source of Information About Resources

We routinely asked respondents about whether they had received briefings on Army resources at that installation during their in-processing to the installation. This question drew negative comments from many respondents across the installations. First, the extent and quality of an in-processing briefing on resources appeared to vary. Respondents mentioned inconsistencies in the orientation processes at different installations in terms of the organizations and services introduced to newly arrived soldiers, noting that soldiers may not learn of specific services until months after they arrive. Some soldiers and spouses reported not receiving a proper welcome or orientation at all. However, other respondents described structured briefings with presentations given by resource provider organizations. From respondents' stories about resource use, it seems that the quality of the in-brief and orientation process—or lack thereof—when a soldier arrives at a new installation can have far-reaching effects on the life of the soldier and his or her family, as it can be the starting point of successful engagement with Army resources or a missed opportunity for getting soldiers engaged with potentially useful services.

A downside to information about resources being presented during in-processing is that the high volume of information seems to detract from soldiers' ability to absorb it. For example, respondents described the briefings with phrases such as "shotgun blast" and "fire hose." Multiple respondents used the phrase "death by PowerPoint" when talking about in-processing. Respondents were pointing to a substantial limitation of a bulk presentation of information during a busy week: soldiers may be unable to take in so much new information in a way that will be useful to them down the road.

On the other hand, there were some positive reviews from soldiers of the in-brief presentation on resources, including some concession that although they might not have remembered exact details of phone numbers or building locations, the in-processing briefing may have a role in creating awareness that a range of resources exist, so that a soldier might recall that *a* resource exists, if not which specific one is appropriate for a problem that emerges down the road. Finally, and not surprisingly, based on the comments we heard from resource providers, those *providing* information during these initial briefings did not seem to have the same negative views held by those on the *receiving* end.

Other Sources of Information About Resources

Other sources of information named by respondents focused on more traditional print and related advertising, such as flyers and printed newsletters. MWR and ACS print publications (e.g., monthly guide to events) were mentioned by a handful of respondents across installations. Respondents at Fort Gordon noted the large, digital billboards on the side of the road near one of the main gates as a place that they had heard about activities or events. Respondents at Fort Meade made reference to flat-panel televisions or monitors that were mounted in the dining facilities as a place to get the word out about resources, because many people move through the space every day. A few service providers expressed the belief that print and other traditional forms of advertising services were better suited to older consumers, and that younger soldiers and spouses preferred social media. However, in the focus groups, younger respondents seemed to mention print and related advertising (e.g., digital billboards) as a potential source of information as much as older respondents, although all respondents described using the Internet and related search resources the most when seeking out information about specific resources.

Perceived Barriers to and Facilitators of Resource Use

Limited Hours

When focus group participants were asked what the biggest barriers were for using on-post resources, they responded by saying that the biggest problem was that they have the same exact duty hours that the soldiers do. In their words, "It comes down to whether or not leadership will let you use those resources." This means that even if the soldiers and their families are aware of the resources, the real challenge is getting to these resources during their hours of operation. They agreed that the resources on post are very helpful when they are able to use them but maintained that these resources are often underused because of the fact that soldiers in particular do not have the time to use them.

Soldiers across the four installations further expressed their frustration with the hours of operation of services on post. They specifically mentioned the big problem this creates for childcare because some day care services on post are not open during early morning PT and will close before all soldiers are off work. At Fort Gordon, someone mentioned having to pay $5 for every minute a child is left at day care past closing time at 6:00 p.m. This creates an additional burden on soldiers who have to coordinate on-post day care and hire a babysitter to cover any time gaps between the day care's closing and the time they get off work. Respondents had similar complaints for other services offered on post (e.g., pharmacy, financial counselors, and auto shop services) that were too busy during lunch to assist everyone and closed before the soldiers were out of work. Some focus groups mentioned this was a problem with the dining facilities as well, which further limited the number of food options. Soldiers admitted to missing class, asking chain of command for permission to miss part of the day, or skipping lunch to make it to service providers during their hours of operation. Soldiers argued that the resources are not meeting the needs if they are not accommodating to the soldiers' work schedules. Participants concurred that the hours of operation for services on post should be based on soldier availability and not interfere with the times they are asked to be at training or doing their job. One participant asked, "If all the soldiers are required to be in PT in the morning, whom exactly are the civilians servicing on base for those first couple hours in the morning?" and another added that "there is just a major scheduling mismatch that causes problems, and frustration, and inefficiency." Soldiers repeated that services on post need to be more soldier-centric and operate during hours that work for soldiers since their primary focus should be to support the soldier.

Some suggestions were that since the Army and civilians are not required to have the same work shifts at the same time, civilians should change their working hours to align with the soldiers. They proposed dispersing the civilian work shifts so that services are available outside the standard business hours of 9:00 a.m. to 5:00 p.m. Other soldiers recommended that services be open one Saturday each month, as they saw at another installation, to allow soldiers to make more use of resources. Providers also spoke of hours as something that they tried to address. Some resource providers specifically mentioned purposefully trying to meet soldiers where they are—literally: attending installation events held outside "typical" work hours and even trying to be available and present in soldiers' work locations (e.g., military and family life counselors or ACS at dining facilities or community events).

Lack of Knowledge on Available Resources

Soldiers and spouses alike pointed to a lack of knowledge about available resources as one of the key challenges they face. Particularly at installations where soldiers may arrive one by one, a comprehensive orientation or introduction to garrison resources may not always happen. Soldiers' lack of knowledge of resources creates repercussions for their spouses and families as well. The lack of knowledge about available resources was the single greatest barrier to spouses' use of resources.

As spouses are not typically included in formal orientation meetings when new families arrive at installations, they are often forced to rely on their soldiers for information. Moreover, Army spouses mentioned the lack of knowledge of available resources as the single greatest challenge for finding and using resources. As a participant in Huachuca stated, "Newly arrived spouses just have no idea where to go and what the [Army-specific] language is or what's happening around here [on post]." As previously mentioned, some families are new to the military, and spouses have a hard time adjusting to the organizational language and military culture, but the transition is most challenging when they do not have a good understanding of the resources available to them. Focus group participants mentioned that the expectation is for units to share information with the soldiers and have them pass this along to their spouses and families, yet it appears that they often do not do this. Spouse respondents reported that some soldiers are just too preoccupied with their roles and responsibilities as soldiers to communicate about this with their families, and others simply refuse to share their spouses' contact information with providers. Hence, rather than spouses learning about the available resources directly, some spouses said that they rely on their soldiers to ask someone for them where they can go when any given problem arises. In soldier, spouse, and service provider focus groups, participants acknowledged that the general model of the soldier being a conduit for Army services information for his or her family works for most families and for many resources, but that the lack of redundancy in this arrangement—where the soldier is a de facto gatekeeper of information about Army services—can be a barrier to spouses and families accessing resources. Spouse participants in particular, as well as some service providers, suggested that inviting spouses to in-briefing services and providing information directly to spouses would be helpful to Army families in which the soldier fails to relay information about Army resources. As a service provider said, "It is critical that people know who to ask and where to ask; they help you when you ask for it."

Challenges with Reaching Soldiers and Family Members

Service providers mentioned a range of challenges in trying to provide resources and in reaching out to soldiers and family members. In terms of limitations cited, providers stated how soldiers' and family members' prior negative experiences with resources could sometimes be a challenge. More broadly, providers noted that help-seeking could at times be stigmatized and cited that as a potential barrier to resource use. For example, some soldiers spoke of being hesitant to reach out to leadership (who in turn could potentially link them with other resources) for this reason and expressed concerns about lack of support and perceptions that their challenges would no longer be private. Some more-senior soldiers noted this as an issue as well.

In addition to stigma surrounding seeking some resources and the limited availability of funds and staff to provide programming, service providers raised communicating with Army spouses and family members as a major challenge for delivering resources. As noted earlier, service providers in particular were challenged by not being able to communicate directly with spouses and often having to use their soldiers as the imperfect conduit for information.

One group that particularly struggled with communicating with spouses was the FRG representatives, who are not technically resource providers themselves but are still part of the system of support.[15] Those members participating in the focus groups voiced their grievance with not being given the spouse or family information they need to reach out to them directly and inform them of opportunities to engage with and learn from other Army spouses. They expressed how this can be particularly difficult for families of soldiers who work in units that prohibit them from discussing their work (e.g., soldiers working with classified or otherwise highly sensitive information), because the inability to talk about work creates a greater disconnect within those families.

In addition to not being able to contact Army spouses, the FRG struggles with an unfavorable reputation. A few FRG representatives admitted having bad experiences themselves with FRGs at previous installations and maintaining a negative opinion about the group until deciding to participate in their current groups. They said that there is such a strong stigma associated with the group that they have to avoid calling their events "FRG events" or spouses might not show up. Despite these challenges, a few leaders showed their determination and willingness to change the image of the group, because they consider themselves to be a crucial resource for spouses, especially during deployment periods.

---

[15] The FRG is an Army commanders' program designed "to provide activities and support that encourage self-sufficiency among its members by providing information, referral assistance, and mutual support" (U.S. Department of the Army, 2013, p. 16).

Role of Partnerships

Next, we discuss the role of installation partnerships to help support soldiers and families. Since the provision of both Army and community resources can involve partnerships between Army and community organizations, partnerships can play an important role in addressing the needs of soldiers and their families.[16] This analysis is somewhat different from the preceding analyses and findings, which are based exclusively on survey data and focus group data acquired in the course of this study. As both survey and focus groups purposefully focused on soldier and family challenges, and Army partnerships were not the primary focus, for this analysis we also drew on the broader military installation partnership literature, other RAND installation partnership research, and interviews with program staff, as well as ancillary discussions during and after systematic data collection related to the study of soldier and family problems and needs at garrison.

Army installations have been implementing public-to-public partnerships and public-private partnerships for many decades. These have been growing in importance for a variety of reasons, including new authority to create public-to-public partnerships,[17] which has resulted in more emphasis on and opportunities for installation and community partnerships. More opportunities for partnerships have also been created as communities have developed around Army installations and the numbers of potential community partners have increased. Furthermore, more soldiers and their families are living off post than in the past and are using more community resources to help meet their needs, as was reflected in the survey findings.[18]

One of the most significant reasons for the increased emphasis on installation partnerships, however, is that budgets at Army installations are declining, and partnerships create the ability to leverage funding, expertise, and capacity to save money in providing some installation soldier and family support, as well as other installation services. For example, a respondent in a service provider focus group or interview at Fort Meade stated that with challenges and declines in installation resources, installa-

---

[16] In its most basic definition, an installation partnership is when an installation and one or more other organizations agree to work together for mutual benefit. A partnership usually involves a long-term relationship and high levels of trust and communication. An installation public-to-public partnership is an agreement between an installation and a local, state, or other federal agency, and a public-private partnership is an agreement between an installation and a private entity, including a company or a nonprofit organization. See Lachman, Resetar, and Camm, 2016, esp. pp. 5–6, for more details about the different types of partnerships.

[17] More authority has been given to military installations to partner with communities because of the passage of Section 331 in the 2013 National Defense Authorization Act. Section 331 (refined in Section 351 of the 2015 National Defense Authorization Act) provided additional statutory authority for military installations to enter into agreements with local and state governments for installation support services, called intergovernmental support agreements.

[18] For more information about the other reasons partnerships have become more important for military installations, see Lachman, Schaefer, et al., 2013.

tion partnerships are a creative way to help provide soldiers and families services. Moreover, installations and communities now have a greater understanding of the range of potential installation and community partnership benefits, including, among others (see Lachman, Resetar, and Camm, 2016, for an in-depth discussion),

- improved military mission
- economic benefits, including cost savings, earnings, and cost avoidance
- improved installation and community operations, facilities, infrastructure, workforce, and services
- additional capacity in resources, skills, expertise, facilities, and infrastructure
- improved strategic regional collaboration
- improved government and community relationships
- enhanced outreach to military personnel and their families and communities.

Key Partnership Areas to Help Meet Soldier and Family Needs

Some key partnership areas that are significant in meeting soldier and family needs were discussed in the focus groups, interviews, and literature. We have grouped these issues into four functional areas (family advocacy, law enforcement, health, and children's issues) based on installation and community organizations. However, it is important to note that installation partnerships are important in other functional areas (including recreation, adult education, libraries, and housing)[19] to help meet soldiers' and family needs as well. We focus here only on a few.

Family Advocacy and Social Services

Army installations' ACS includes the Family Advocacy Program (FAP). The Army FAP seeks to prevent domestic violence and abuse, prevent child neglect and abuse, protect victims of sexual assault and abuse, and, jointly with U.S. Army Medical Command and medical treatment facilities, treat victims and offenders. The FAP uses a coordinated community approach to support soldiers and families in an attempt to prevent relationship problems and family violence among installation personnel. Related to that aim, for domestic violence and spouse abuse, installations tend to rely on partner help for items such as emergency shelter services, crisis hotlines, and other victim services. For example, Fort Benning has partnered with the Columbus Alliance for Battered Women, Inc., and the Crisis Center of Russell County for information sharing, coordination of services, training on each other's policies and procedures (including military requirements), educational outreach to the local community, and victim advocacy. The partners provide emergency housing for military spouses, their children, and female soldiers who are victims of abuse or sexual assault (Fort Benning, n.d.a; Fort Benning, n.d.b). A few focus group and interview respondents echoed asser-

---

[19] For more information about other installation partnership types that help support soldiers and their families, see Lachman, Resetar, and Camm, 2016.

tions about the importance of partnerships for providing emergency shelter services and other family advocacy services, including at Fort Hood and Fort Gordon. Thorny interrelated problems faced by soldiers and their families may require coordination with additional community resources, ranging from law enforcement to medical care, in order to help achieve solutions.

Law Enforcement: Safety, Security, and Supporting Soldiers

The literature on installation partnerships and some of the respondents in the focus groups and interviews of service providers stressed the importance of partnerships and having good connections and working relationships with local and regional law enforcement, such as at Fort Huachuca and Fort Hood. Such respondents included Provost Marshals, FAP managers, medical and mental health providers, garrison leadership, and civilian leaders. Installations often have law enforcement partnerships that involve training together or sharing resources (personnel, equipment, and vehicles) related to law enforcement and police services, such as relying on a partner for a special weapons and tactics team or bomb squad help. In some cases, the installation is relying on the community for help, and in others it is vice versa, depending on which organization has the capacity for the region. This offers dividends in terms of the general safety of the community.

Partnerships in law enforcement can also involve information sharing, especially about when soldiers and family members are in trouble with the law or in cases in which local law enforcement is trying to help prevent soldiers from getting in trouble. For example, one respondent from Fort Hood stated that police from Austin, Texas, contact staff at Fort Hood if a soldier is involved in family abuse or some type of assault at a hotel or club. Similar statements were made by participants at other site visits; these less formal types of interactions may often be supported by the presence of formal partnerships that enable installation and community members to develop trust. In another example, a Killeen, Texas, police officer responding to an incident involving a soldier who is having severe emotional problems might call on the Fort Hood Resiliency Campus for assistance.

These partnerships, some formal and some informal, can be supported by a regular schedule of communication and working together. For instance, Fort Gordon has over 50 memoranda of understanding with different law enforcement agencies throughout the state for a variety of purposes. Having regular monthly meetings, whether formal or informal, was cited by respondents as a way to help develop and maintain a close working relationship between installation and civilian law enforcement, especially when there is staff turnover.

Medical and Mental Health

Installation partnerships are also important for providing health care to soldiers and their families. In fact, respondents in focus groups and interviews at several installations stressed the importance of partnerships for health care. Given the reliance on civilian health care providers for many specialty areas at many installations (through TRICARE), health care collaboration and partnerships are quite prevalent. Health care is a complex system on both the military and the civilian sides, and it varies based on location and the populations and medical resources available in a region. For example, Fort Huachuca is in a primarily rural area with limited medical facilities in the community, and for some specialty care, soldiers and their families have to drive 1.5 hours to Tucson for care because the resources are not available in the local area, as noted in at least one focus group. As another example, Fort Meade is within the National Capital Region, which has a variety of both military and civilian medical treatment facilities and health care resources available, though, as noted in Meade focus groups, reaching them can mean braving traffic congestion. Given the wealth of medical resources in the region, Fort Meade does not have an Army hospital and instead relies on its TRICARE partner, HealthNet. As stated by a Fort Meade health care service provider in an interview, Fort Meade health care service providers have a good working relationship with civilian providers and include them in their network.

Other types of partnerships include medical education and training partnerships, which often focus on military medical staff being trained in the community through individual classes at hospitals, in specialized training programs, and in trauma centers, and civilian health care providers conduct training in garrison facilities. For example, a respondent at Fort Meade stated that they perform joint training of nurses in partnership with the community. Some installation medical training partnerships focus on improving certain medical capabilities within the region, such as training more psychological professionals to be able to provide mental health services to military personnel and their families (Clampett, 2012).

Children's Issues

Installation and community partnerships related to children are also important for helping to meet the needs of soldiers and families. The focus of these partnerships range from the community partner helping with childcare, school activities, or after school activities for military children, to soldiers helping children at activities and schools in the community. For example, there are installation partnerships that focus on helping Army soldiers and their families with the kinds of childcare issues raised in focus groups (e.g., limited operating hours and the expense of services). Childcare partnerships focus on sharing, operating, and facilitating access to or maintaining childcare facilities, as well as helping provide before- and after-school care to military children. For example, in a partnership at Fort Bragg, a nonprofit organization, Partnership for Children of Cumberland County, helps Army families find access to affordable and quality childcare. In fact, some Fort Bragg families' children attend the Spainhour Center at little or no cost to the families because this center receives funding from the partnership through its programs designed to help prekindergarten-age children and the U.S. government because of the number of military children who attend it.[20]

---

[20] A grant from the Department of the Army's National Association of Child Care Resource and Referral Agencies also helps cover some of the costs associated with this childcare. For more information, see Fitzgerald and

Installation and Community Partnership Best Practices

We will now discuss three installation partnership best practices for helping to meet soldier and family needs, based on our analysis of the focus group and interview responses, the literature, and related ongoing partnership work at RAND.

The first best practice we note is creating and maintaining a good relationship with the community. Some service provider respondents highlighted the importance of having a close working relationship with the community that helps meet soldier and family needs, and they noted that a close working relationship with the community in turn helps to develop and grow both formal and informal partnerships.[21] One respondent at Fort Huachuca said that a good working relationship with the local community was especially important for them since they are a smaller post and do not have as many resources and cannot offer as many services to soldiers and families as can some other, larger installations. Thus, they must rely on the community for more services, suggesting that the community and installation have a vested interest in each other's success.

Another best practice is proactive collaboration to help prevent a soldier or family member from having a problem or making a problem worse. These types of prevention activities often emerge from informal partnerships with different parts of the community, especially law enforcement. The examples, discussed earlier, of local police contacting installations about problem soldier behaviors illustrate this point. Other examples of proactive partnerships with off-post business organizations were mentioned by two or three service providers in the focus group and interviews at Fort Gordon and Fort Hood, especially with respect to housing issues and efforts to make sure soldiers are not taken advantage of by unscrupulous businesses.

Last, monthly or other regularly scheduled installation and community events held by functional service provider counterparts, whether formal or informal, were identified by respondents as a best practice because they help develop good and proactive working relationships between installations and communities. These were mentioned in the context of law enforcement earlier, but other functional areas where regular meetings have been mentioned as important include health care, mental health, schools, adult education, and chaplain services. For example, a chaplain who was interviewed at Fort Hood and had been previously stationed at Fort Stewart mentioned how they had a quarterly meeting with civilian clergy in the region surrounding Fort Stewart. This meeting was called the Church Relations Forum, and it provided a venue for local clergy to meet Fort Stewart chaplains and learn about resources available to their congregants. These meetings helped local clergy learn about how soldiers and their families struggle with post-traumatic stress disorder and other war-related emotional issues and the resources available to help them (for more information, see Fort Stewart, 2012).

Paraglide, 2010.

[21] For more information, see, for example, the discussion on page 7 of Lachman, Resetar, and Camm, 2016.

CHAPTER FOUR

Summary Findings and Recommendations

The Army provides an array of quality-of-life support services for soldiers and their families, but, until recently, it has lacked a holistic assessment of problems soldiers and families face and what types of assistance they believe are needed to confront and solve those problems (Sims, Wong, et al., 2013; Sims, Trail, et al., 2017). Thus, our data help to fill a key gap in the Army's understanding of challenges faced, perceived needs, and resources used: that of soldier and family perceptions. Information on these specific topics was collected by means of a unique Army-wide survey in which soldiers reported the types and range of problems they and their families faced, and what types of help they felt they needed to deal with those problems. Army-wide analyses and methodology of the survey are presented in detail elsewhere; this report focuses on a more local examination: the garrison level. Although not all CONUS garrisons surveyed supplied sufficient data to be examined in depth, many did. We supplemented this quantitative survey work with qualitative data collection to high-light local dynamics and illuminate the process of how soldiers cope with the challenges they face, within the context of garrisons selected based on profiles of problems, needs, and resource use from the survey results. This approach enabled us to explore the topic areas highlighted by the survey methodology in greater depth, as well as to gather the perspectives of Army spouses and service providers on the challenges faced by soldiers and families and, in some cases, what solutions might be appropriate.

While our data fill a key gap, it should be noted that they are not the only relevant information. For example, both our quantitative and our qualitative approaches speak to what soldiers and families perceive they need, rather than what helping profession-als may prescribe. Moreover, these data do not speak to the available information on use of and satisfaction with resources by the general population and the Army (and relevant trends), population demographics, or cost and benefit considerations. A wealth of other research and information exists on soldiers' and families' experience of Army life, in terms of both the challenges faced and the use of and satisfaction with services and programs available to alleviate those challenges, albeit without the unique focus provided by our approach (see our overview of this research in Sims, Trail, et al., 2017, as well as other overviews available, such as Segal and Harris, 1993; McClure, 1999; OSD, 2004; Booth, Segal, and Bell, 2007; and OSD, 2009).

Although our data speak to Army averages (and averages at the garrison level of analysis) in perceived challenges and needs, and they are supplemented by qualitative depth, they do not fully resolve the challenge of gauging the essentiality of programs and services that have relatively low uptake but are vital to those who do need them; one example of this is the Exceptional Family Member Program. And although the focus groups and interviews offered the opportunity for discussion of what soldiers and families perceived the Army as doing well, they did not explicitly address challenges that would arise in the absence of a given resource—that is, the discussion focused on the current situation faced by soldiers and families rather than asking the counterfactual of what soldiers and families would need the most help with if all resources were removed. Issues presenting as relatively minor in the current environment could become major challenges in the absence of existing Army supports. However, if changes are implemented, our data would serve as an important baseline.

How Garrison Leaders and Service Providers Can Use This Report

Areas where there are differences across garrisons suggest that the local context plays a role in the challenges soldiers and their families face. Differences among garrisons might suggest that a local solution is needed or that the local context, including initiatives by leaders, may help soldiers and their families successfully address the challenges they face. The comprehensive and systematic approach taken by the survey enables leaders to make decisions about garrison needs and priorities based on empirical data describing the Army population. This study provides unique information that enables service providers and garrison leadership to understand where they are doing well in relation to other surveyed garrisons, where their communities still report experiencing challenges in addressing their most pressing problems effectively, and where additional effort might be warranted.

What We Found

Garrison Problems Generally Reflected Those at the Army Level

With regard to the survey analysis by garrison, prioritized problem areas chosen by soldiers at a local level reflected the earlier Army-level analysis: Military Practices and Culture, Soldier's Well-Being, and Work-Life Balance were chosen the most frequently. The focus groups generated a rich discussion of the types of problems soldiers and their families face, which covered somewhat different ground from the survey results. This difference in part reflected the different focus of the discussions, which were more an exploration of the process of coping with different problems than an attempt to prioritize only problems that were the most challenging in the prior year. Thus, focus groups spoke to military practices and culture, work-life balance, and soldier well-being, but health care and childcare system problems were also frequently mentioned. Quite often, neither the survey findings nor the focus groups spoke to a particular type of problem being localized. Rather, our findings illustrated that certain problems are typical, regardless of location. The finding regarding pressing problems echoes other work that has found that military life, and in particular deployments and demands of duty days, can pose challenges for servicemembers (e.g., Sticha et al., 1999; Booth, Segal, and Bell, 2007; Karney and Crown, 2007; Posard, Hultquist, and Segal, 2013).

Although the problem domains most frequently chosen by soldiers were largely the same across garrisons, there was significant variance in the selection of some specific problem domains. For example, compared to the average, Health Care System Problems was more frequently chosen as a top problem by respondents at Fort Meade, was ranked as one of the top three problems chosen by Fort Meade respondents, and was frequently mentioned by focus group respondents at Fort Meade. In addition, although Military Practices and Culture was ranked as a top problem across garrisons, it was chosen more frequently by respondents at Fort Bragg, compared with the average. Similarly, Work-Life Balance ranked as a top concern for almost all garrisons, but it was chosen more frequently at Fort Hood, compared with the average. Thus, although our findings illustrated that certain problems are typical, regardless of location, some significant variation in the prevalence of these problems among soldiers occurred across garrisons.

Garrison Findings Reflected More Variability in Types of Help Needed

In contrast to the survey findings regarding problems, where overall findings were often generally similar across garrisons, more variability in the types of help needed was evident at the garrison level. When asked what kinds of help they needed to cope with their most pressing problems, the needs for advice, activities, and general information were all fairly common among soldiers across garrisons. The need for advice was common, and a desire for interpersonal assistance can be seen as associated with that need, as can needs for counseling, emotional support, or an advocate at several garrisons. For example, at Meade the need for an advocate was more frequently chosen as a top need compared to average, and it was often cited as a need for dealing with problems related to military practices and culture. Overall, the specific types of needs reported by soldiers at different garrisons varied, but activities, information, and help provided by an actual person—through advice, counseling, or advocacy—were the most common needs reported by soldiers.

We did not seek specific information regarding types of help needed in the focus groups, because we felt that information would be revealed in the discussion of problem solving and resource use, which we did pursue in depth. However, we noted that those discussions did not reveal needs for any particular types of problem-solving help that were simply unavailable; rather, challenges related to barriers to accessing and using the help needed.

Soldiers at Different Garrisons Often Sought Help in Different Ways

The vast majority of respondents reported using a variety of military and nonmilitary resources to address their needs. Furthermore, with the exception of Fort Leavenworth, where soldiers used fewer Army resources than average, the number of Army and non-military resources used did not differ by garrison. However, garrisons varied on which resources were used most frequently. For example, compared to the average, soldiers at Fort Meade were more likely to use the chain of command and unit members not in the chain of command as resources, whereas soldiers at Forts Eustis and Polk were less likely than average to use their chain of command as a resource. Fewer than 20 percent of respondents at any garrison reported that their needs were unmet (that is, that the resources they reached out to met their needs in a manner rated less than "all right"), and compared to the average, soldiers at Fort Polk were less likely to report unmet needs. The results of the focus groups suggest that some military resources are particularly helpful across garrisons, including chaplains and ACS. However, focus group respondents were less consistent in reporting the helpfulness of other military resources, such as the chain of command.

Some Tension Exists Between a Desire for Resilience and a Desire to Seek Help

Focus group findings also shed light on the process of resource seeking. They brought to light a tension between a desire for self-sufficiency or resiliency in problem solving and a desire to seek help. That is, soldiers at all levels often reported that they wanted to be able—or should be able—to solve their problems themselves without needing to bring leadership into the equation. That sentiment was balanced by the responses of NCOs who expressed a sense of responsibility for their soldiers, along with an awareness that soldiers might wish to maintain their privacy. Respondents pointed out that the downside of this tension can be that, by the time individuals realize they are in over their heads and need assistance, their challenges have evolved into a much knottier problem to untangle. In addition, focus groups with spouses and service providers revealed that spouses are often uninformed about the resources available to help them. Service providers highlighted challenges in getting access to spouses—including the lack of contact information for spouses—to provide spouses with accurate information about the resources available to them.

Problem Areas Tend to Be Interconnected

Focus group discussions of soldier problems also revealed that many problems are interconnected. For example, many respondents spoke of today's "24-hour Army" and the need to do more with less, both challenges relating to Work-Life Balance. These spilled over into Soldier's Well-Being because soldiers were unable to both manage a home life and make as much progress as desired with regard to professional life due to a lack of time. Military Practices and Culture challenges exacerbated these issues: as more taskings and requirements were piled on, they were seen as contributing to a lack of time to develop relationships with soldiers and foster the ability to provide advice. This was particularly felt by midlevel leadership responsible for answering both to those up the chain and for the well-being of soldiers under them. Another point of discussion was the promotion of soldiers who had not had time to develop as leaders themselves. These soldiers were seen as inadequate for the task, either because they did not feel appropriately responsible for their soldiers or because they were unskilled in the work of forging bonds. Respondents noted that, coupled with time pressure, inexperienced leadership could diminish effective and strategic problem solving at all levels, further exacerbating workload challenges.

Soldiers Use a Variety of Methods to Find Out About Resources to Solve Their Problems, but Barriers to Accessing Resources Were Still a Challenge

Our focus groups revealed that soldiers use a variety of methods to find out what resources they have at their disposal, ranging from social media to more "traditional" sources such as word of mouth (including advice from NCOs). In fact, the Internet and word of mouth were the most common modes of finding out information. Focus group discussions about the barriers to accessing resources suggested that lack of knowledge, lack of experience with resources, and limited hours of operation were commonly perceived barriers to resources. Other challenges included soldier uncertainty on when accessing resources would trigger unit involvement, which most junior soldiers wanted to avoid. One best practice that seemed to work well was being able to get accurate, useful referrals to needed resources from convenient contacts such as the garrison ACS office and NCOs. To facilitate this, service providers spoke of keeping up to date on what resources were available for a variety of problems, even those outside the scope of their office's services. That way, they could serve as points of referral when someone came to them with a problem they could not solve with only the service they offered. Overall, it was clear that ACS, NCOs, and chaplains played key roles in connecting soldiers to resources.

What We Recommend

We offer the following recommendations for things the Army should do or should consider doing. As our findings reiterate the presence of challenges identified by other work as well (e.g., Castro, Adler, and Britt, 2006; Booth, Segal, and Bell, 2007; Miller et al., 2011), we draw from the literature where appropriate.

Some Garrisons Need to Take Specific Actions to Address Challenges

Our survey findings suggest that while the general menu of Army services is meeting the majority of needs, specific garrisons need to pay greater attention to the particular needs expressed and resources used by their soldiers. The need for some type of interpersonal help—such as advice, counseling, social support, or advocacy—was expressed across most garrisons, with soldiers at Meade indicating a particular need for an advocate. This suggests that resources providing one-on-one, personalized help should be given priority—especially at Fort Meade—and it is possible that emphasizing trust between soldiers and their leaders could help fulfill this need. More generally, the need for information was widely prioritized across installations, with soldiers at Bragg indicating a particular need for specific information. This suggests that providing easily accessible information online (as this was reported as one of the primary sources sought for information on what is available), for example, and staffing services that provide information to soldiers and their families should be continuing priorities for the Army as a whole and particularly at Fort Bragg.

Practices That Enhance Partnerships Can Help Meet Soldier and Family Needs

Army garrisons should consider focusing more in their intergovernmental support agreements and other community partnership activities on partnerships that help meet soldier and family needs, as these partnerships offer a creative way to address some of the challenges faced. The partnership best practices discussed in this report highlight ways in which installation personnel can best take advantage of opportunities. To do this, the Office of the Assistant Chief of Staff for Installation Management, Installation Management Command Headquarters, and Army garrisons should encourage installation personnel to develop close working relationships with relevant civilian agency personnel in areas such as social services, law enforcement, health care, mental health, religious organizations, recreation, and schools. They should also encourage installation personnel to develop more proactive partnerships, including informal ones, to help prevent soldier and family problems in relevant areas. To help foster and maintain these types of relationships, installation functional personnel in key areas should be encouraged to hold regular events with relevant civilian functional personnel (similar to the best practice noted among installation personnel of keeping informed of and in touch with each other). Such regular interactions could be informal social events or more formal meetings held monthly, every other month, or quarterly; the key element is having a regular schedule to facilitate communication. Some installations are already doing many of these things, but more could be done, especially at installations that may not have close working relationships with their communities.

The Army Might Consider a Series of Solutions to Achieve the Right Balance Between Fostering Resilience and Helping Its Soldiers Solve Problems Early

One solution is to expose NCOs and other soldiers earlier and more frequently in their careers to information regarding what resources are available. Shorter, more frequent exposure may provide better opportunities for the information to sink in and for integrating information into routines (Burke and Hutchins, 2007; Brown and Sitzmann, 2011), especially given the complexity of the information and the task of helping soldiers and families (e.g., Noe, 2008). We are not suggesting yet another training requirement, which would create even more of a time burden for soldiers and leadership (see

Wong and Gerras, 2015, for a discussion of the proliferation of training requirements and its negative consequences). Rather, we are suggesting taking advantage of existing systematic opportunities to provide the information, such as routine in-processing or counseling sessions.

Another solution is to set priorities at the aggregate Army level, given the time available to soldiers, rather than leaving it up to lower levels to determine which of the many requirements passed down they must prioritize. As noted in the literature, leaders must prioritize activities they consider necessary (e.g., Schein, 2004; Fernandez and Rainey, 2006; Wong and Gerras, 2015). This requires a more strategic approach and an admission of the difficulties of balancing all the requirements of today's Army. A frank appraisal of priorities and time commitments at the highest levels and conveyed to lower levels may help accomplish tasks that are otherwise not allotted enough time, such as NCOs' establishment of trust with their soldiers. As noted in *Army Leadership* (U.S. Army, 2012), building trust is an essential leadership competency.[1] Indeed, our results suggest that this is important at all levels in setting the stage for soldiers to work with their NCOs, and establishing trust between junior soldiers and NCOs should be prioritized as well. Furthermore, focus group findings point to the need for NCOs and junior officers to be guided in their development as leaders, perhaps by providing them with examples of senior leaders who are exemplars for the skills required to lead an Army in garrison.

The Army Should Consider Strengthening the "No Wrong Door" Policy at Army Community Service and Broadening the Policy to Help Soldiers and Families Navigate Resources

Focus group participants identified NCOs and particular programs and services as gateways to finding more targeted assistance to address their problems. The suite of programs under ACS already have a "no wrong door" policy that states, "No matter to whom Soldiers and Family members talk with or where they seek services, they have come to the right place" (Lynch, 2010), and chaplains are also a dependable conduit to other resources. Enabling leadership and other programs and services to fulfill this navigation assistance role and instructing them on how to carry out this policy would make help seeking more efficient for soldiers and their families. The goal would be to ensure that both leadership (e.g., NCOs) and all program personnel who provide services to soldiers and family members are trained to direct them to the appropriate resource for their problem, even if the resource is outside their program office.

This would involve making sure that leaders know about the services available to soldiers and family members, and that the individual programs and services in the portfolio know about each other, potentially through training or education of program

---

[1] More generally, trust is often considered integral in developing a plan of action for mental or physical health issues and following it; see, for example, the literature on treatment adherence summarized by Krueger, Berger, and Felkey, 2005.

personnel. Any offered education might be opened to FRG leaders as well to increase the reach of the no wrong door policy. The specific roles and duties of each entity under the no wrong door policy should ideally be codified so that each knows its responsibilities. For example, regulations should specify whether the hand-off between programs should be passive (e.g., telling a soldier about a different program that could help him or her) or active (e.g., calling the program and setting up an appointment for the soldier).

Part of the goal of this solution is to ensure that the existing gateways to more targeted assistance, namely, ACS and the chaplain service, remain available to soldiers and their families. This includes continuing to fund the resources and services that reliably meet needs. These resources may also offer an advantage in terms of relative privacy to the extent that problems confessed, and assistance given, are not reported back to the units. While it is true that this makes it more difficult for unit leaders to monitor problems, given the desire on the part of soldiers to solve problems on their own and privately, and the desire of NCOs and others to facilitate resilience, the Army should seriously weigh the pros and cons of allowing greater confidentiality.

In Conclusion, Striking a Balance Is Essential

The Army needs its soldiers, many of whom are very young and new to the responsibilities of adulthood, to keep their personal lives on an even enough keel to maintain readiness and their ability to deploy. Deployments can be uniquely challenging work events as well. The Army has an interest in helping soldiers maintain their personal lives to facilitate their professional ones. That said, the Army also has an interest in promoting resilience among its force, which by definition involves facing difficulties and coping with them successfully. However, inexperience with challenging situations can lead to problems in one domain that can spill over into other domains and become even more difficult to handle. In some ways, the Army has set up a system designed to handle this challenge particularly for junior enlisted soldiers: the NCO corps. However, some challenges currently render this system less than optimal (see Langkamer Ratwani et al., 2012; Shanker, 2014).

One challenge we heard described by focus group respondents is a changing culture that in some ways places greater emphasis on privacy, making it more difficult for NCOs to bond with soldiers and create an environment that fosters asking for help when it is necessary. NCOs also reported relatively little time to build relationships, given the impetus to do more with less and accomplish all of the many taskings. For example, we heard that mandatory training requirements exceeded the available training time (see review in Wong and Gerras, 2015). We offer a number of suggestions in this report to help the Army strike the right balance between addressing problems proactively and allowing for the inevitable mistakes that come with allowing soldiers and their families to develop resilience.

Soldier Self-Management of Problems Focus Group Protocol

Respondent Groups
- junior enlisted single soldiers
- junior enlisted soldiers with dependents
- NCOs
- officers.

Objectives
- Gauge participant knowledge of resource environment, how they currently get information about resources, and what suggestions they have for making resource information more readily available to soldiers.
- Understand what barriers, beyond resource awareness, keep soldiers from accessing resources, and what resource providers and others (e.g., leadership) can do to help soldiers overcome these barriers.
- Gather explanations of multiple resource use.
- Gauge awareness and use of civilian or community resources to meet needs.
- Assess the extent to which chain of command is seen as and used as a resource to help with soldiers' problems.

Room Setup
Include a wall poster or handouts listing problems, needs, and resources taken from survey.

Introduction
Good [morning or afternoon]. [Introductions of facilitator and note takers. Description of recording setup. Discussion of informed consent and ground rules.]

Description of Problems, Needs, and Resources
Before I start off with my questions, I want to tell you a little more about what we're studying and define some terms, so that we're all on the same page.

We're interested in how soldiers deal with and overcome the challenges that people face in everyday life. We have a list of the types of problems we're talking about on the [wall/printout], and you can see that although we'll use the word *problem*, these are really a wide range of the things that people deal with. Some of them might be a big deal and some might be resolved quickly and easily.

What you might need to solve a problem could be a range of things, depending on the situation. We're calling these *needs*. They are on the [wall chart/handout]. For example, if you're having a problem with your health care, you may want advice from someone with more experience (e.g., if you're making a choice about how to treat a health problem), or you might just need more information (e.g., about what procedures are covered for dependents).

The Army is concerned about soldier and family well-being, and about problems that become distractions or liabilities and get in the way of unit readiness. That's why the Army provides many resources to support soldiers in their professional and personal lives. When we talk about *resources*, we mean the list of things on the [resources list/poster], things like recreation facilities and programs, childcare and family support programs, spiritual support, and medical care. We'll be talking mostly about resources that the military provides.

To understand how the problems and needs of soldiers match up with Army resources, we first conducted a survey of soldiers that asked about common problems and the types of resources they used. We want to talk to you today to learn more about how and why soldiers use or don't use the different types of resources available. We're also interested in if and how Army resources are meeting soldiers' needs, and what they can do to be more effective. In our conversation, we're primarily going to be asking about your experiences at this installation. However, if at certain points you think it would be helpful to tell us about experiences from other installations, please be sure to mention where they occurred so our notes are accurate.

Demographics

First, I'd like to start by going around and learning a little bit about you, just to find out how long each of you have been in the Army, how long you have been at this installation, and what your Military Occupational Specialty is. Can I get a show of hands for . . . single? Married? Kids? Deployments?

Thanks. That's really helpful to get an idea of whom we're talking with today.

1. Looking at this list, which problems would you say are the most common for soldiers like you?

Resource Environment

2. For those who have needed help with these types of problems in the past year, what Army resources did you turn to for help?
   a. What resources
   b. How find out
      i. When soldiers like yourselves want to take advantage of Army resources, how do you figure out where to go? (probes: ask peers; ask commander;

web research; one-stop telephone line; ask program that already have contact with; bulletin boards; resource centers)

1. Is there a centralized webpage that lists resources?
2. Have you ever been given a list of resources, like in a manual?
3. Is there a point of contact, either for this installation or in your unit, that is designated as a go-to person for getting information about resources?
4. What's the best way to get information to soldiers about the resources that are available at [LOCATION]?
5. Was there ever a time when you or someone you know couldn't find a resource to help with a problem? (What kind of problem? What did you/other person do?)

c. Multiple resources

   i. Our survey results suggested that soldiers typically contact five to six different resources when trying to resolve a particular problem. We're trying to understand what this might mean. One possibility is that people are bouncing around from place to place trying to identify the appropriate resource. Another possibility is that the first resource they contact is the correct one, but they don't like it or it fails to help them. Another possibility is that soldiers tackling complicated issues are simply having different needs met at different places.

   ii. Can you think about examples of where you or people you know ended up contacting many different resources in an effort to address one type of problem? What was going on in those cases?

d. Quality

e. Barriers

   i. Suppose a soldier had a problem and knew about an installation resource designed to help people with just that sort of thing [like if his family was having a problem with childcare and he knew about Child and Youth Services/like if he was looking for things to do in his off-duty time and he knew about MWR]. Can you think of any reasons why a soldier might *not* use a program or resource? (probe barriers only if not raised: time/location conflicts, hard to actually get access, stigma/don't want to be seen as a program user, program/resource has bad reputation, better nonmilitary alternative)

   ii. Have you heard about soldiers having bad experiences with any of the resources on this installation, or had bad experiences yourself? What did they experience? (probe only if not mentioned: not helpful, insensitive, long waits, inconvenient) [For each complaint, get expectation of realistic wait time, services, access, etc.]

        iii. When you think about Army resources that have good reputations, or that soldiers have good experiences with, what are those programs or resources doing right? (probe best practices: no wrong door, good information, respectful, discreet, responsive)

  f. [Listen for mapping onto major problems and prompt for resources for common problems that haven't been mentioned.]

  g. Are there any nonmilitary resources that you've heard of people using? If so, why use these over Army resources? (probes if not already raised: closer to home, perceived higher quality/greater effectiveness, shorter wait time, privacy/confidentiality, spouse preference)

  h. Chain of command as resource

        i. For what types of problems and needs, if any, do you think your chain of command might be a good resource for help? Why or why not? And, just as a reminder, we won't be reporting your responses to your chain of command, and we ask that you respect one another by not sharing each other's opinions outside this group.

        ii. Based on what you know, do they seem to have the *expertise or ability* to help soldiers with their problems?

        iii. Do they seem to have the *time* to help enlisted soldiers?

        iv. Do they seem like they *want* to help? What gives you that impression?

  i. What about unit members outside the chain of command? For what kinds of problems and needs might you turn to them and why?

  j. Are there problems that you would definitely not take to the chain of command? Why? (e.g., problems wouldn't be well received, could negatively impact career, too personal/embarrassing, chain of command not qualified [e.g., medical issues], the problem is with the chain of command)

  k. If the chain of command is one place you can turn to for help when you have problems, where would you turn if you felt your chain of command was actually a source of or contributor to the problem? As examples, what would you do if your immediate supervisor gave you an unfair performance evaluation or was being abusive to subordinates?

3. Anything about [location] with regard to problems or resources available that you think makes this installation unique?

Conclusion

Those are all of the specific questions we have today. Before we go, though, I'd just like to see if anyone has any parting thoughts for us to consider as we learn how soldiers go about addressing the different problems and needs that inevitably arise as a part of everyday life. Is there anything in particular we spoke about today that you would like to emphasize, or anything we didn't discuss that we should be sure to think about?

    Thank you for your time.

References

Army Strong Bonds Program, "Stronger Relationships Mean a Stronger Army," March 1, 2017. As of March 27, 2017:
https://www.strongbonds.org/skins/strongbonds/home.aspx

Bello-Utu, Cindy F., and Janiece E. DeSocio, "Military Deployment and Reintegration: A Systematic Review of Child Coping," *Journal of Child and Adolescent Psychiatric Nursing*, Vol. 28, No. 1, 2015, pp. 23–34.

Booth, Bradford, Mady Wechsler Segal, and D. Bruce Bell, *What We Know About Army Families: 2007 Update*, Washington, D.C.: U.S. Department of the Army, Family and Morale, Welfare and Recreation Command, 2007.

Brown, K. G., and T. Sitzmann, "Training and Employee Development for Improved Performance," chapter 16 in S. Zedeck, ed., *APA Handbook of Industrial and Organizational Psychology*: Vol. 2, *Selecting and Developing Members for the Organization*, Washington, D.C.: American Psychological Association, 2011, pp. 469–503.

Burke, L. A., and H. M. Hutchins, "Training Transfer: An Integrative Literature Review," *Human Resource Development Review*, Vol. 6, 2007, pp. 263–296.

Castro, Carl Andrew, Amy B. Adler, and Thomas W. Britt, *Military Life: The Psychology of Serving in Peace and Combat*: Vol. 3, *The Military Family*, Westport, Conn.: Praeger Security International, 2006.

Clampet, Jennifer, *WBAMC Collaborates to Attract Psychology Intern*, El Paso, Tex.: Fort Bliss Monitor, 2012.

Fernandez, S., and H. G. Rainey, "Managing Successful Organizational Change in the Public Sector," *Public Administration Review*, Vol. 66, No. 2, 2006, pp. 168–176.

Fitzgerald, Paula M., and Paraglide, "Partnership for Children Helps Fort Bragg Community," *U.S. Army*, March 12, 2010. As of August 24, 2017:
https://www.army.mil/article/35764/partnership-for-children-helps-fort-bragg-community/

Fort Benning, "Memorandum of Understanding Between the Army Community Service (ACS) Family Advocacy Program (FAP) Fort Benning, Georgia and Crisis Center of Russell County," n.d.a.

———, "Memorandum of Understanding Between the Army Community Service (ACS) Family Advocacy Program (FAP) Fort Benning, Georgia and the Columbus Alliance for Battered Women, Inc.," n.d.b.

Fort Stewart, "Church Relations Forum," information paper, December 8, 2012.

ICF International—*See* Inner City Fund International.

Inner City Fund International, *2012 Army MWR Services Survey—Army Report*, Fairfax, Va.: ICF International, 2012a.

———, *2012 Army MWR Services Survey—Workforce Category Report*, Fairfax, Va.: ICF International, 2012b.

Jennings, B. M., L. A. Loan, S. L. Heiner, E. A. Hemman, and K. M. Swanson, "Soldiers' Experiences with Military Health Care," *Military Medicine*, Vol. 170, No. 12, 2005, pp. 999–1004.

Karney, Benjamin R., and John S. Crown, *Families Under Stress: An Assessment of Data, Theory, and Research on Marriage and Divorce in the Military*, Santa Monica, Calif.: RAND Corporation, MG-599-OSD, 2007. As of July 16, 2018:
https://www.rand.org/pubs/monographs/MG599.html

Krueger, P. Kem, Bruce A. Berger, and Bill Felkey, "Medication Adherence and Persistence: A Comprehensive Review," *Advances in Therapy*, Vol. 22, No. 22, July/August 2005, pp. 319–362.

Lachman, Beth E., Susan A. Resetar, and Frank Camm, *Military Installation Public-to-Public Partnerships: Lessons from Past and Current Experiences*, Santa Monica, Calif.: RAND Corporation, RR-1419-A/AF/NAVY/OSD, 2016. As of July 16, 2018:
https://www.rand.org/pubs/research_reports/RR1419.html

Lachman, Beth E., Agnes Gereben Schaefer, Nidhi Kalra, Scott Hassell, Kimberly Hall, Aimee E. Curtright, and David E. Mosher, *Key Trends That Will Shape Army Installations of Tomorrow*, Santa Monica, Calif.: RAND Corporation, MG-1255-A, 2013. As of July 16, 2018:
https://www.rand.org/pubs/monographs/MG1255.html

Langkamer Ratwani, Krista, Kara L. Orvis, Kerri Conning Chik, Tiffany Poeppelman, Stephen J. Zaccaro, and Jeffrey E. Fite, *NCOs Leading in Garrison: An Investigation of Challenges and Leadership Requirements*, Arlington, Va.: U.S. Army Research Institute for the Behavioral and Social Sciences, 2012.

Lynch, Rick, "Services Delivered, Promises Kept," *The Real McCoy Online*, December 10, 2010. As of August 24, 2017:
http://www.mccoy.army.mil/vnewspaper/newspaper/realmccoy/12102010/d6_sends.htm

Mansfield, Alyssa J., Jay S. Kaufman, Stephen W. Marshall, Bradley N. Gaynes, Joseph P. Morrisey, and Charles C. Engel, "Deployment and the Use of Mental Health Services Among U.S. Army Wives," *New England Journal of Medicine*, Vol. 362, No. 2, 2010, pp. 101–109.

McClure, P., ed., *Pathways to the Future: A Review of Military Family Research*, Marywood, Pa.: Military Family Institute, 1999. As of November 3, 2011:
http://handle.dtic.mil/100.2/ADA364886

Meadows, Sarah O., Laura L. Miller, and Jeremy N. V. Miles, *The Association Between Base-Area Social and Economic Characteristics and Airmen's Outcomes*, Santa Monica, Calif.: RAND Corporation, RR-132-AF, 2014. As of July 16, 2018:
https://www.rand.org/pubs/research_reports/RR132.html

Meadows, Sarah O., Laura L. Miller, Jeremy Miles, Gabriella C. Gonzalez, and Brandon Dues, *Exploring the Association Between Military Base Neighborhood Characteristics and Soldier and Airman Outcomes*, Santa Monica, Calif.: RAND Corporation, TR-1234-RC/A/AF, 2013. As of July 16, 2018:
https://www.rand.org/pubs/technical_reports/TR1234.html

Military Health System, *Final Report to the Secretary of Defense: Military Health System Review*, Falls Church, Va.: Defense Health Agency, 2014.

Miller, Laura L., Bernard D. Rostker, Rachel M. Burns, Dionne Barnes-Proby, Sandraluz Lara-Cinisomo, and Terry R. West, *A New Approach for Assessing the Needs of Service Members and Their Families*, Santa Monica, Calif.: RAND Corporation, MG-1124-OSD, 2011. As of July 16, 2018:
https://www.rand.org/pubs/monographs/MG1124.html

Noe, Raymond A., *Employee Training and Development*, New York: McGraw-Hill Irwin, 2008.

Office of the Secretary of Defense, *2004 Quadrennial Quality of Life Review*, 2004.

———, *2009 Quadrennial Quality of Life Review*, 2009.

OSD—*See* Office of the Secretary of Defense.

Posard, Marek N., Marc Hultquist, and David R. Segal, "Adjusting the Duty Day Schedule to Improve Health and Family Life in Garrison," *Journal of Human Behavior in the Social Enviornment*, Vol. 23, No. 6, 2013, pp. 789–799.

Schein, E. H., *Organizational Culture and Leadership*, 3rd ed., San Francisco: Jossey-Bass, John Wiley & Sons, 2004.

Segal, Mady Wechsler, and Jesse J. Harris, *What We Know About Army Families*, Special Report 21, Alexandria, Va.: U.S. Army Research Institute for the Behavioral and Social Sciences, 1993.

Shanker, Thom, "After Years at War, the Army Adapts to Garrison Life," *New York Times*, January 18, 2014.

Sims, Carra S., Thomas E. Trail, Emily K. Chen, and Laura L. Miller, *Assessing the Needs of Soldiers and Their Families*, Santa Monica, Calif.: RAND Corporation, RR-1893-A, 2017. As of July 16, 2018:
https://www.rand.org/pubs/research_reports/RR1893.html

Sims, Carra S., Anny Wong, Sarah H. Bana, and John D. Winkler, *Strategically Aligned Family Research: Supporting Soldier and Family Quality of Life Research for Policy Decisionmaking*, Santa Monica, Calif.: RAND Corporation, TR-1256-A, 2013. As of July 16, 2018:
https://www.rand.org/pubs/technical_reports/TR1256.html

Sticha, Paul J., Robert Sadacca, Ani S. DiFazio, C. Mazie Knerr, Paul F. Hogan, and Marisa Diana, *Personnel Tempo: Definition, Measurement, and Effects on Retention, Readiness, and Quality of Life*, Alexandria, Va.: U.S. Army Research Institute for the Behavioral and Social Sciences, 1999.

Troxel, Wendy M., Regina A. Shih, Eric R. Pedersen, Lily Geyer, Michael P. Fisher, Beth Ann Griffin, Ann C. Haas, Jeremy Kurz, and Paul S. Steinberg, *Sleep in the Military: Promoting Healthy Sleep Among U.S. Servicemembers*, Santa Monica, Calif.: RAND Corporation, RR-739-OSD, 2015. As of March 20, 2017:
http://www.rand.org/pubs/research_reports/RR739.html

U.S. Army, *Army Command Policy*, AR 600-20, Washington, D.C.: Department of the Army, 2014.

———, *Army Leadership*, ADRP 6-22, Washington, D.C.: Department of the Army, 2012.

U.S. Department of the Army, *Military Morale, Welfare, and Recreation Programs and Nonappropriated Fund Instrumentalities*, Army Regulation 215-1, Washington, D.C.: U.S. Department of the Army, Morale, Welfare, and Recreation, 2010.

———, *Army Regulation 608-1 Personal Affairs: Army Community Service*, Washington, D.C., 2013.

Wong, Eunice C., Lisa H. Jaycox, Lynsay Ayer, Caroline Epley, Racine Harris, Scott Naftel, and Susan M. Paddock, *Evaluating the Implementation of the Re-Engineering Systems of Primary Care Treatment in the Military (RESPECT-Mil)*, Santa Monica, Calif.: RAND Corporation, RR-588-OSD, 2015. As of March 20, 2017:
http://www.rand.org/pubs/research_reports/RR588.html

Wong, Leonard, and Stephen J. Gerras, *Lying to Ourselves: Dishonesty in the Army Profession*, Army War College Carlisle Barracks, Penn.: Strategic Studies Institute, 2015.